Political Economy

Providing a 'short take' on the long history of political economy, this book examines both the stories *about* and those *within* economics. It traces the history of political economy from its beginnings in the Scottish Enlightenment; through its disciplinary demarcation as a science in the nineteenth century that saw its differentiation from literary, aesthetic, and moral discourses; and to its emergence as the 'amoral' market-driven neoliberalism that dominates economic theories and policies today.

In exploring the long history of economic thought, it examines and challenges both Enlightenment and contemporary grand narratives such as the stadial theory of progress, the 'Great Divergence', and the 'Great Convergence' that have divided the world into global norths and souths according to their economic advantages. It concludes with a study of currency as both a medium of monetary exchange and a term that denotes prevalence and acceptance to explore political economy's continuous engagement with the problem of representing value through money.

Part of the series *Short Takes on Long Views*, this book will appeal to a traditional academic audience of scholars and students and to a wider public audience of informed non-fiction readers interested in the long history of economics.

Sarah Comyn is an Assistant Professor and Ad Astra Fellow in the School of English, Drama and Film at University College Dublin. She is the author of *Political Economy and the Novel* (2018) and co-editor of *Worlding the South* (2021).

Short Takes on Long Views
Series Editors: Peter Otto, Clara Tuite, and Elias Greig

Contemporary notions of reason, imagination, literature, science, sexuality, democracy, Nature and even the Human were forged by Enlightenment and Romantic thought. Yet this inheritance now seems unseated by developments it has helped engineer: the digital revolution, globalisation, climate change, fake news, and the emergence of artificial intelligence.

In this time of rapid change, *Short Takes on Long Views* aims to re-address and re-envision the founding of modernity, its contemporary legacies, and the multiple futures. The series puts the so-called "universal" ideas of the European Enlightenment (and subsequent Romantic responses and revisions) into a global context to transform their histories and legacies in the present, and to imagine new possibilities for the future.

Short Takes on Long Views presents small books on big questions, which will to appeal to both researchers and students across the Humanities and Social Sciences.

Enlightened Aboriginal Futures
Barry Judd and Katherine Ellinghaus

Political Economy
Sarah Comyn

For more information about this series, please visit: www.routledge.com/Routledge-Handbooks-in-Religion/book-series

Political Economy

Sarah Comyn

LONDON AND NEW YORK

First published 2025
by Routledge
4 Park Square, Milton Park, Abingdon, Oxon OX14 4RN

and by Routledge
605 Third Avenue, New York, NY 10158

Routledge is an imprint of the Taylor & Francis Group, an informa business

© 2025 Sarah Comyn

The right of Sarah Comyn to be identified as author of this work has been asserted in accordance with sections 77 and 78 of the Copyright, Designs and Patents Act 1988.

All rights reserved. No part of this book may be reprinted or reproduced or utilised in any form or by any electronic, mechanical, or other means, now known or hereafter invented, including photocopying and recording, or in any information storage or retrieval system, without permission in writing from the publishers.

Trademark notice: Product or corporate names may be trademarks or registered trademarks, and are used only for identification and explanation without intent to infringe.

British Library Cataloguing-in-Publication Data
A catalogue record for this book is available from the British Library

ISBN: 978-1-032-25115-8 (hbk)
ISBN: 978-1-032-25116-5 (pbk)
ISBN: 978-1-003-28162-7 (ebk)

DOI: 10.4324/9781003281627

Typeset in Times New Roman
by Apex CoVantage, LLC

For Luke and Kit

Contents

List of Figures	*viii*
Acknowledgements	*ix*
Introduction	1
1 Courting the Imagination	7
2 Grand Economic Narratives	33
3 Currency	51
Index	*69*

Figures

I.1 *Three of Diamonds* [South Sea Bubble Playing Cards]. London: Carrington Bowles, 1721. Kress Collection (Bancroft). 2
I.2 *Jack of Hearts* [South Sea Bubble Playing Cards]. London: Carrington Bowles, 1721. Kress Collection (Bancroft). 3
1.1 £20 bank note featuring Adam Smith. The author's own photograph. 8
3.1 James Gillray, *Midas, Transmuting all into Paper*, London 1797. © The Trustees of the British Museum. Used with permission. 52
3.2 George Cruikshank, *Bank Restriction Note*, London, 1819. © The Trustees of the British Museum. Used with permission. 53

Acknowledgements

I would like to thank Elias Greig, Peter Otto, and Clara Tuite for their generous invitation to be a part of this exciting and innovative series. My heartfelt thanks to Clarice Ballenden, Corinna Box, Gayle Comyn, and Miriam Nicholls for their astute and careful reading. At Routledge, I would like to thank Georgia Oman and Lucy Batrouney for their kindness early in the process and Payal Bharti for her patience and assistance in the final stages. I would also like to thank colleagues at University College Dublin for their ongoing support and encouragement, in particular: Emma Bennett, John Brannigan, Danielle Clark, Lucy Cogan, Nicholas Daly, Fionnuala Dillane, Katherine Fama, Porscha Fermanis, Jane Grogan, Megan Kuster, Pedzisai Maedza, Michelle O'Connell, Nicolas Pillai, and Emilie Pine. For their constant championing, special thanks to Alison Garden, Kathryn Milligan, and Fariha Shaikh. Finally, my deepest gratitude is to Anthony Assad.

Introduction

Following the South Sea Bubble crash in 1720, satirical playing cards were circulated depicting those who had invested deeply and those who had equally lost their fortunes in the speculative financial scheme founded on the trade of enslaved people. As gaming cards, these satirical cards captured the gamble inherent to the South Sea scheme and mocked those who fell for it. The Three of Diamonds (Figure I.1), for instance, portrays a Lady pawning her rich jewels, only to sink all her funds in the scheme such that she has to replace all her fine stones with fakes, while the Jack of Hearts (Figure I.2) rejects a former lover who had spurned his attentions when her gambles were paying off, but who suspiciously came courting again as soon as her South Sea stocks plummeted.

Almost 300 years later, in 2016, shortly before the launch of the new Jane Austen £10 note, the micro-engraver Graham Short engraved 5mm portraits of Austen onto four £5 notes before spending and putting them into circulation in Scotland, England, Wales, and Northern Ireland. As the public became aware of these special, engraved notes and began actively looking for them, the value of these £5 notes quickly skyrocketed to approximately £50,000. Because their unique serial numbers included Austen's year of birth, even some of the new £10 Austen notes reportedly sold for thousands of pounds as banknote evaluators began speculating and advising punters about which serial numbers could attract the most money.

Though separated by three centuries, these instances of circulating paper capture the imaginative character of their economies: they imagine and embody excess, speculate about fluctuating value, and highlight the frequent disconnect between representative and actual value. They emphasise the gamble attached to economic stories, while themselves telling and selling their own economic story. Exploring the long history and evolution of political economy from the eighteenth century to the virtual economics of today, this book studies exactly these sorts of moments of imaginative, literary, and economic intersection. It argues that despite the discipline of economics' frequent historical attempts to regulate and deny the influence of narrative in favour of abstraction and mathematical calculations, fiction has always been implicit in

DOI: 10.4324/9781003281627-1

2   *Introduction*

Figure I.1 *Three of Diamonds* [South Sea Bubble Playing Cards]. London: Carrington Bowles, 1721. Kress Collection (Bancroft).

Figure I.2 *Jack of Hearts* [South Sea Bubble Playing Cards]. London: Carrington Bowles, 1721. Kress Collection (Bancroft).

economic theory and is traceable to the very origins of political economy in the Scottish Enlightenment.

A turn to narrative and the stories circulating about economics has newly caught the attention of many prominent economists. In a lecture delivered at the London School of Economics in 2019, for example, the Nobel prize-winning economist Robert J. Shiller began with what he described as the 'audacious claim' that a revolution was underway within the economics and financial professions: the transformation of macroeconomic theory through the recognition and incorporation of *narratives*.[1] Despite Shiller's express wish to identify a revolutionary impulse within contemporary economic theory, his account of 'narrative economics' ignores the origins of economics in eighteenth-century political economy, rhetoric and moral philosophy. Nor is Shiller the only economist who has turned to the explanatory power of narratives to re-examine the intellectual, social, and political history of economics. Recent financial crises, such as the Global Financial and Eurozone crises, have prompted public and scholarly reflection on the history of economics as a discipline and the significant role it plays in everyday life. Diagnosing the failures of the economics profession following the 2008 Global Financial Crisis, another Nobel prize-winning economist, Paul Krugman, wrote that economists 'mistook beauty, clad in impressive-looking mathematics, for truth'.[2] The economist and scholar Deirdre McCloskey was already arguing in the 1990s that 'the economist, like a novelist, uses and misuses stories'.[3]

Providing a 'short take' on the long history of political economy, this book examines both the narratives *about* and those *within* economics. It traces the history of political economy from its beginnings in the Scottish Enlightenment; through its disciplinary demarcation as a science in the nineteenth century that saw its differentiation from literary, aesthetic, and moral discourses; and to its emergence as the 'amoral' market-driven neoliberalism that dominates economic theories and policies today. In exploring this long history of economic thought, it examines and challenges both Enlightenment and contemporary grand narratives such as the stadial theory of progress, the 'Great Divergence', and the 'Great Convergence' that have divided the world into global norths and souths according to their economic advantages.

This book is divided into three chapters that explore the crucial elements defining political economy: origins, narratives, and mediums of exchange. With its focus on the intersection of economics with the literary, aesthetic, and ethical discourses of its origins, it should be quite clear already that this is not your traditional 'introduction to economics'. We will not be investigating the origins or efficacy of GDP, for example, nor will we be debating the role of stagflation in the modern economy. We will, however, be studying the disciplinary history of economics, a history that the profession of economics often wilfully chooses to ignore, despite the continued impact this history has in shaping the achievements and failures of economics as a discipline and profession.

I: Courting the Imagination

The first chapter explores the origins of political economy in Enlightenment moral philosophy and the process by which it became recognised as a science in the nineteenth century. This section examines the literary, aesthetic, and moral discourses that influenced and challenged the work of political economists such as Adam Smith, Thomas Malthus, David Ricardo, Karl Marx, J. S. Mill, and William Stanley Jevons, and twentieth-century economists such as John Maynard Keynes, Friedrich von Hayek, and Milton Friedman. Paying attention to this history of the transformation of political economy reveals the legacy of the aesthetic within contemporary economics.

II: Grand Economic Narratives

The second chapter of this book studies the implications of the Eurocentrism of the major 'stories', epistemologies, and ontologies of economics—such as stadial theory, *homo economicus*, the Industrial Revolution, and the Great Divergence—and the challenges to these narratives that have been posed by behavioural economics, feminist economics, and postcolonial economic theorists. This chapter ends with a discussion of the current grand narrative of the 'Great Convergence', how this is reshaping the political economy of the global 'north', and the counternarratives being encouraged by proponents of degrowth.

III: Currency

The final chapter focuses on currency as both a medium of monetary exchange and a term that denotes prevalence and acceptance to explore political economy's continuous engagement with the problem of representing value through monetary forms: from bills of exchange, to paper money, to virtual currencies like Bitcoin. This chapter explores the romantic and mythological narratives that both demonstrate and elide the representational nature of currency and how these narratives are impacting the financial markets of today. Looking at the causes of and responses to crises such as the Bank Restriction Act of 1797, the Global Financial Crisis, and the rise and fall of cryptocurrencies, this concluding chapter considers the models of financial literacy advocated by political economists and how this literacy is dependent on the training provided by literary and aesthetic discourses.

Notes

1 Robert J. Shiller, 'Narrative Economics', *London School of Economics*, 6 September 2019. See also, Shiller's recent book of the same name, *Narrative Economics: How Stories Go Viral and Drive Major Economic Events* (Princeton: Princeton University Press, 2019).

6 *Introduction*

2 Paul Krugman, 'How Did Economists Get It so Wrong?', *New York Times Magazine*, 2 September 2009, https://www.nytimes.com/2009/09/06/magazine/06Economic-t.html
3 Deirdre McCloskey, *If You're So Smart: The Narrative of Economic Expertise* (Chicago: Chicago University Press, 1990), 1.

1 Courting the Imagination

The origins of modern economics can be traced to the Scottish Enlightenment and Adam Smith's magnum opus, *An Inquiry into the Nature and Causes of the Wealth of Nations* (1776). Consisting of five books and over a thousand pages, Smith's *Wealth of Nations* explored and introduced topics, the significance of which continue to be investigated today: the division of labour, the free market, and the character of *homo economicus*—the rational self-interested individual making economic decisions that unintentionally regulate the market.[1] While Smith has long been recognised as the father of modern economics, what is often ignored in this identification of Smith as a landmark political economist is Smith as a moral philosopher, rhetorician, and theorist of jurisprudence. All four of these categories of knowledge are crucial to understanding Smith's writing, philosophy, and influence.[2]

As a rhetorician, Smith was keenly aware of the power of language and stories in narrating, explaining, and demonstrating economic principles. His opening chapter begins by situating his reader in the pin factory in order to illustrate the division of labour:

> One man draws out the wire, another straights it, a third cuts it, a fourth points it, a fifth grinds it at the top for receiving the head; to make the head requires two or three distinct operations . . . and the important business of making a pin is, in this manner, divided into about eighteen distinct operations.[3]

Though 'a very trifling manufacture', Smith is then able to magnify his pin factory analogy to capture 'every other art and manufacture' and demonstrate how the division of labour increases the 'productive power of labour' across all trades.[4]

Immortalised and brilliantly represented on the £20 note (Figure 1.1, 2007–2020), Smith's division of labour demonstrates and performs the systematisation and structuring of economic knowledge.[5] Witness, he asks his readers, the performance of a fundamental economic principle in the creation of one of the smallest and most 'trifling' objects. Consider then, what this

DOI: 10.4324/9781003281627-2

8 *Courting the Imagination*

Figure 1.1 £20 bank note featuring Adam Smith. The author's own photograph.

division could achieve if working at a larger scale. The imagination and narration are crucial to Smith's success in illustrating these economic principles as scaleable: 'A system is an imaginary machine, invented to connect together in the fancy those different movements and effects which are already in reality performed'.[6] Like the structures of the pin factory, the causes and circulations of the wealth of a nation can be understood as a system whose movements and effects we connect through the imagination.

Consider how Smith builds on his example of the pin factory by following an object—a woollen coat—out of the factory of production and into the worlds of exchange: 'as course and rough' as the day-labourer's woollen coat may be, it is nonetheless the product of the combined labour of 'the shepherd, the sorter of the wool, the wool-comber or carder, the dyer, the scribbler, the spinner, the weaver, the fuller, the dresser, with many others'.[7] A common product encountered in everyday life, Smith's woollen coat becomes an analogous economic artefact: he uses it as a means of illustrating how the complexities of the nation's economic system are actually traceable in ordinary lives, and in doing so, appeals to his readers' imagination. Having already noted a distinction between the number of labour subdivisions possible in manufacturing versus agriculture, Smith introduces the day-labourer's woollen coat as a way of uniting these two industries and then demonstrates how the division of labour naturally leads to exchange, which finally allows him to advocate for the free market. Each form of labour demarcated by the commas in the sentence quoted earlier is also potentially a moment of exchange as they take their distinct labour through their product into the market: 'Every workman has a great quantity of his own work to dispose of . . . he is enabled to exchange a great quantity of his own goods for a great quantity . . . of theirs'.[8] The connection between the division of labour and the free market of exchange that Smith has established through his analogies of the pin factory and the woollen coat is then reinforced by his characterisation of human nature as defined by 'the propensity to truck, barter, and exchange'.[9] This tripartite composite of human nature allows Smith to naturalise exchange and the division of labour, implicitly introduce the stadial theory of progress, and embody his most famous metaphor: the invisible hand of the market.

Though only explicitly making an appearance once in Book IV of *The Wealth of Nations*, the invisible hand is crucial to Smith's thesis as a whole: the market operates most efficiently when not interfered with because when we pursue our own interests, we 'frequently promote' the interests of society 'more effectively than when [we] really intend to promote it'.[10] Smith does not need to introduce and name the invisible hand earlier in this work because his metaphoric accounts—such as the circulating labour in the woollen coat (which also embodies our natural propensity to truck, barter, and exchange)—are enacting his economic model. While a normative account of how Smith thinks the economy should operate, through the process of reading *The Wealth of Nations*, Smith's model becomes naturalised and normalised in such a way that by the time the reader encounters the invisible hand, it is already the perfect explanatory tool for his wider economic narrative.

Smith, however, first planted the seed of the invisible hand in his treatise on moral philosophy, *The Theory of Moral Sentiments* (1759), demonstrating the importance of reading the two works together rather than as distinct disciplinary endeavours. Here, the invisible hand is even more pointedly connected to the imagination, as it is in a discussion of the ability of the imagination to keep industry in motion that he introduces this powerful metaphor. It is a two-step process: first 'our imagination[s]' 'naturally confound' objects and products such as the woollen coat or pin so that we are struck by the 'order, the regular and harmonious movement of the system, the machine or economy by means of which [they are] produced'. Building on this systematic power of the imagination—what Smith portrays as the 'deception which rouses us and keeps in continual motion the industry of mankind'—Smith then argues that the rich are

> led by an invisible hand to make nearly the same distribution of the necessaries of life, which would have been made, had the earth been divided into equal portions among all its inhabitants, and thus without intending it, without knowing it, advance the interest of the society.

Captivated by the harmony achieved by the economic system, our imaginations (according to Smith) in combination with our self-interested actions, allow for an orderly distribution of wealth and trade. Finally, Smith's conclusion of this point seemingly embodies the power of the imagination to deceive through the autonomous order it achieves, as he argues: 'In ease of body and peace of mind, all the different ranks of life are nearly upon a level, and the beggar, who suns himself by the side of the highway, possesses that security which kings are fighting for'.[11] The lyrical turn of the sentence here and the comparative imaginative excess in aligning beggars with kings displays in full the deceptive power of the imagination. As McCloskey noted: economists use and misuse stories.[12]

While Smith is most noted for his figuration of the invisible hand which seemingly codifies self-interest as the most efficient operating force in an 'amoral' market economy, this version of Smith dismisses the attention he paid to the individual's relationship with and *within* society. Smith's *Wealth of Nations* developed out of a series of lectures on jurisprudence which he described as 'that science which inquires into the general principles which ought to be the foundation of the laws of all nations'.[13] Crucially, Smith defines the science of political economy as 'a branch of the science of statesman or legislature'; one that 'proposes both to enrich the people and the sovereign'.[14] Here, he imagines a political economic system that enriches people financially, socially, and morally. The version of Smith's work and philosophy as synonymous with the celebration of the individual also ignores that as a moral philosopher and a theorist of jurisprudence, he created a second, much-celebrated metaphorical figure: the impartial spectator who *imaginatively* divides themself in two in order to judge their behaviour and the behaviour of others. Drawing on a tradition of moral spectators from the work of philosophers David Hume and Francis Hutcheson, Smith endeavours to find and maintain a balance between self-interest and a flourishing society (financially, culturally, and morally). The metaphorical figures of the impartial spectator and the invisible hand, therefore, need to work cooperatively in order for individuals to discover the 'most advantageous employment' for capital and to become mediating moral actors. In uniting these figures, Smith not only relies on the active engagement of the imagination, but he makes a literary intervention too: he populates his philosophical treatises with metaphoric figures that seemingly become characters—the impartial spectator, the wheel of circulation, the invisible hand—that the reader can join on a narrative journey through the economic systems defining the wealth of nations.

Naturalising Abstract Political Economy

Unlike Smith, David Ricardo's stylistic approach to political economy in his *On the Principles of Political Economy and Taxation*, published in 1817, is defined not by metaphor but by abstraction. Ricardo tries to define political economy as a distinctive science by repeatedly separating himself from the descriptive and imaginative language in the *Wealth of Nations*. In contrast to the Smith's imaginative setting of the pin factory, Ricardo's language is categorical and invites a calculative approach from the beginning of his Preface: 'The produce of the earth—all that is derived from its surface by the united application of labour, machinery, and capital, is divided among three classes of the community, namely, the proprietor of land, the owner of the stock or capital necessary for its cultivation, and the labourers by whose industry it is cultivated.'[15] In this opening passage, Ricardo repeatedly uses categories of three to develop a uniting calculation of division for his readers: produce is created through three categories of application (labour, machinery, and capital), which is then divided among three classes (landowner, capitalist, labourer) according to three categories of payment and wealth (rent, profit, and wages). Understanding the 'laws' that govern the distributive connections between these tripling categories is the purpose of political economy according to Ricardo. Rather than inhabiting the imaginative factory or following the day-labourer's coat, we, as readers of Ricardo, are already analysing the distribution of wealth according to abstract categories and classes. While Smith, too, is concerned with the distribution of wealth, his foundational definition of political economy identifies its objectives as:

> provid[ing] a plentiful revenue or subsistence for the people, or more properly to enable them to provide such a revenue or subsistence for themselves; and secondly, to supply the state or commonwealth with a revenue sufficient for the public services.[16]

There is a discourse of responsibility attached to Smith's definition that is lost in Ricardo's abstraction. The abstract and categorical character of Ricardo's writing is further evident in a passage where Ricardo is 'estimating the exchangeable value of stockings'. Stylistically, this passage mimics Smith's coat analogy, but in terms of description and narrative, it is vastly different:

> First, there is the labour necessary to cultivate the land on which the raw cotton is grown; secondly, the labour of conveying cotton to the country where the stockings are to be manufactured, which includes a portion of the labour bestowed in building the ship . . . thirdly, the labour of the spinner and weaver.[17]

What may at first appear as a simple distinction—the replacement of an identifiable worker (for example, the spinner or weaver) in Smith with the 'labour of . . .' in Ricardo—in fact allows Ricardo to abstract the human element from this calculation, such that the value of stockings is determined by analysing the 'aggregate sum of these *kinds* of labour'. We are no longer imagining the human agents busy in the making of Smith's coat but instead aggregating their abstracted labour. This distinction implies a move away from Smith's jurisprudential and rhetorical political economy towards a scientific account of aggregate sums and facts that will carve a path for the mathematical impulses of neoclassical economics' Marginal Revolution later in the century. The implications of this abstraction of the human *from* labour inspired and concerned many writers, thinkers, and political economists in the nineteenth century.[18] Charles Dickens wrote, for instance, that 'political economy was a mere skeleton' unless it had a 'little human filling or blooming' while the consequences of an abstracted understanding of labour would play a fundamental role in Karl Marx's later critique of capital and political economy.[19]

Ricardo's contemporaries were equally attentive to the implications of this stylistic difference. Thomas Malthus, author of the infamous *An Essay on the Principle of Population* (1798) was concerned by Ricardo's reliance on theoretical models rather than inductions from observations and practical applications. Robert Torrens, another nineteenth-century political economist and author of *An Essay on the Production of Wealth* (1821), shared this concern, but was equally critical of Malthus' deficient analyses that did not match the 'eminent degree' with which he could observe phenomena.[20] These critiques reveal debates about the remits of political economy as well as demonstrating the importance of understanding and analysing political economy as a *genre* of writing. The influence of Ricardo's *Principles* moved political economy from the domain of jurisprudence, moral philosophy, rhetoric, and *narrative* to the *domain of facts*.[21]

The implications of this stylistic and generic move are also traceable in the need for women writers to supplement the abstract and factual writing of the domain of facts with imaginative writing in order to market the philosophy of political economy and make it digestible to a public. Thus, women writers such as Jane Marcet, Maria Edgeworth, and, later, Harriet Martineau were crucial to political economy's ability to imaginatively court the public. Marcet's *Conversations on Political Economy*'s (1816) six editions are testament to the popularity of her approach of 'familiarly explain[ing] the science' through a 'colloquial form' that pays careful attention to the emotions.[22] The development of political economy as a *science* and the distinctions between Smith's and Ricardo's approaches is detectable in the changes in her definitions of political economy in the first two editions of *Conversations*. In the first edition, the teacher, Mrs B., defines political economy as 'the science which teaches us to investigate the causes of wealth and prosperity of nations'.[23] This, of course, echoes Smith's definition. The definition contained in the second edition, however, has Mrs B. explain that 'political economy treats of the formation, the distribution, and the consumption of wealth, it teaches us the causes which promote or prevent its increase, and their influence on the happiness or misery of society'.[24] This definition, in contrast, mimics the abstract triples of Ricardo, through Marcet's use of economic terms such as, 'formation, distribution and consumption'. Marcet is simultaneously careful, however, to ameliorate any negative associations with abstraction through the reference to the emotions and society as a whole. In the *Conversations*, Marcet is performing a complicated balancing act of preserving the figurative (and in many ways, reassuring) elements of Smith, while ensuring that the development of a scientific language of political economy, associated with the likes of Ricardo, continues. The colloquial form also allows Marcet to naturalise the theories of political economy as she stages and controls the debates about the science's remits. When the student, Caroline, gently challenges Mrs B.: 'I think ... you have the art of converting everything you touch into that science'; Mrs B. is adamant: 'It is not my art, but the real nature of things'.[25] The laws governing the formation, distribution, and consumption of society are therefore stabilised as natural fact by Marcet's narrative structure and Caroline's conversion. Marcet's popularity suggests that though imaginative narrative was sidelined in Ricardo's project, it was still necessary for the successful adoption of political economic principles by the public and was always accompanying and working in parallel to the domain of facts.

Ricardo's Exemplary Student

This bifurcation of political economy and imaginative writing is embodied by the political economist who succeeded Ricardo in eminence and is possibly the most famous political economist of the nineteenth century, John Stuart Mill. Mill describes in his *Autobiography* how his father James Mill's instruction in political economy required him (at the age of 13) to

> apply to Smith's more superficial view of political economy the superior lights of Ricardo, and detect what was fallacious in Smith's arguments, or erroneous in any of his conclusions. Such a mode of instruction was excellently calculated to form a thinker; but it required to be worked by a thinker, as close and vigorous as my father.[26]

Trained in the Utilitarianism of his father and Jeremy Bentham, Mill was therefore committed to Ricardo's project of economic abstraction. Acknowledging that the 'conception' of political economy as a 'branch of science' was 'extremely modern', Mill was careful to register the disciplinary boundaries of political economy, arguing that its 'subject is Wealth' and that it makes 'an entire abstraction of every other human passion or motive; except those as antagonizing to the desire of wealth'; it 'has nothing to do with the comparative estimation of different uses in the judgement of a philosopher or of a moralist'.[27] Establishing these 'amoral' remits of political economy allows Mill to build on Ricardo's abstract frame of analysis and further refine the science of political economy.

Like Ricardo, Mill catalogues and aggregates labour in abstraction: as an 'agent of production', labour is either 'directly employed' in the creation of the product or in previous facilitative operations and therefore 'to estimate' the labour involved in the production of 'any given commodity ... is far from a simple one'.[28] Mill's calculative catalogue of the labour involved in making bread, for example, moves from the labour of the baker to that of the miller, to consider the 'labour of the blacksmith who made the plough', devolving to such an extent that he ponders the labour involved in making the 'tools used by the blacksmith, and the tools used in making those tools, and so back to the origins of things'.[29] Here, absurdity lies, however, and Mill acknowledges the limits of this analysis as we move into 'a region of factions too minute for calculation', and therefore, he relies on the abstraction necessary to achieve the 'aggregate sum of labour'. Political economy, Mill argues, requires us to 'always be prepared' to 'shift our point of view, and not consider individual acts, and the motives by which they are determined, but national and universal results'.[30] Yet as with Ricardo, it was exactly these aggregating moves and abstract logic that drew the condemnation of later critics such as John Kells Ingram who dismissed Mill's economic actors as 'imaginary men' who were no more than 'money-making animals'. While Ingram was concerned with the 'just degree of abstraction' necessary for political economy's scientific analysis, Mill would argue that theoretical abstractions were the foundations of the discipline.[31]

As with labour, so with value: 'In considering exchange value scientifically, it is expedient to abstract from it all causes except those which originate in the very commodity under consideration.'[32] Mill's systematic approach to theorising political economy and policing its disciplinary boundaries also had the effect of naturalising its major tenets. In explaining the 'laws of value', Mill writes with the confidence that these laws are already well-established and solved:

> Happily there is nothing in the laws of value which remains for the present or any future writer to clear up; the theory of the subject is complete: the only difficulty to be overcome is that of so stating it as to solve by anticipation the chief perplexities which occur in applying it: and to do this, some minuteness of exposition, and considerable demands on the patience of the reader are unavoidable.[33]

While there is a hint of humble-bragging irony in his reference to the '*only* difficulty' in this passage, Mill nonetheless manages to sweep aside any potential critiques of the theory of exchange value in this declarative and naturalising gesture. Just as Marcet dismissed the student Caroline's questioning of the quotidian nature of political economy, Mill here dismisses any questioning of political economy's factual and causal domain: its laws are not up for debate, *only* how those laws are interpreted and understood.

Despite his demarcative and delimiting abstractions, Mill not only recognised, but himself also needed, the humanistic, sympathetic, and imaginative relief provided by literature, famously writing in his *Autobiography* that the Romantic poets, William Wordsworth and Samuel Taylor Coleridge, assisted him in a fanciful escape from his father's didacticism. Through their expression of 'not mere outward beauty, but states of feelings, and of thought coloured by feeling', Wordsworth's poetry became a 'medicine for [Mill's] state of mind':

> They seemed to be the very culture of the feelings, which I was in quest of. In them I seemed to draw from a source of inward joy, of sympathetic and imaginative pleasure, which could be shared in by all human beings; which had no connection with struggle or imperfection, but would be made richer by every improvement in the physical or social condition of mankind.[34]

While one might argue and dismiss this as a personal expression rather than something relevant to Mill's economic treatises, these 'states of feeling' resonated with him and are traceable in his frequent returns to his *Principles of Political Economy* (first published in 1848), which he repeatedly revised over his lifetime. Because of the effective force of his economic abstractions, it is easy to ignore Mill's attempts to incorporate social philosophy into his political economy, but this intent is stated in the very subtitle of his *Principles*: 'with some of their applications to social philosophy'. Undoubtedly bounded by the clarifying 'some', Mill's efforts to include the study of concerns other than the pursuit of wealth would be influential for economists such as Alfred Marshall and would see him later criticised by neoliberal economists like Friedrich von Hayek for being a socialist.

Capital as Secret

If Mill is the most famous political economist of the nineteenth century, then Karl Marx is political economy's most infamous critic. While Mill quickly moves onto the summative, the aggregate, the seemingly 'universal', Marx lingers on the mysterious, ghostly secrets political economy glosses over. This is not to deny Marx's use of the abstract, which he deploys frequently, acknowledging, for instance at the start of his chapter concerning absolute and relative surplus-value that in 'considering the labour process, we began by treating it in the abstract, independently of its historical forms'.[35] But as this very quote suggests, Marx is always attentive to the implications of the move to abstraction and what it excludes; he does not allow for political economy's theoretical claims to be taken for granted or considered, in the words of Mill, 'complete'. Instead, Marx challenges political economy by turning its own 'logical' premises against itself, as for instance, when he ridicules Nassau Senior's 'last hour'—the notion that capitalists make their profit in the final hour of the working day. Or when he scathingly reduces Mill's account of surplus-value to its most basic premises: 'After thus proving clearly that capitalist production would still continue to exist even if it did not exist, Mill now proceeds, quite consistently, to show that it would not exist even if it did exist'.[36] Marx's writing style provides the supplementary support for his logical attack on political economy. In his style, Marx emphasises the gothic and mysterious and thereby significantly undermines the abstract style of classical political economy.

Marx evokes the secret in one of his most famous chapters, 'the fetishism of the commodity and its secret' which begins by immediately unsettling and defamiliarising what readers might take as 'natural' or mistakenly consider as not worth further analysis:

> A commodity appears at first sight an extremely obvious, trivial thing. But its analysis brings out that it is a very strange thing, abounding in metaphysical subtleties and theological niceties.

Divorced from the labour that produced it, a wooden table *as commodity* is no longer simply a table but

> transcends sensuousness. It not only stands with its feet on the ground, but, in relation to all other commodities, it stands on its head and evolves out of its wooden brain grotesque ideas, far more wonderful than if it were to begin dancing of its own free will.[37]

The sheer excess of Marx's description of the table as commodity here troubles the genre of political economy, electrifying it with jolts of the literary imagination that *de*naturalise the theoretical status quo. Marx, too, uses the coat as an analogy, but it is not simply representational of the cumulative division of labour as we encountered with Smith, rather Marx asks his readers to consider its 'mysteriousness' and what it 'conceals'.[38] Marx, therefore, invites his readers to solve the mystery of capitalism with him.[39]

Interjecting into the accepted narrative of classical political economy that views most of its laws as resolved and only in need of further explication, Marx instead challenges his readers to question political economy's domain of facts. Political economy, for Marx, is not settled, but rather requires decipherment and revelation: 'Value, therefore, does not have its description branded on its forehead; it rather transforms every product of labour into a social hieroglyphic'.[40] Here we are very far away from Mill's claim that the theory of value does not need any 'clear[ing] up'. Marx's gothicisation of political economy undermines its scientific boundaries and appeals to rationality. Marx's version of political economy is, therefore, haunted (by those elements unspoken or glossed over by the classical political economists) and needs discerning readers to reveal its mysteries, not simply trust its 'accepted' rationality. Like Smith, Marx frequently appeals to the imaginative abilities of his readers, but unlike Smith, Marx does not use narrative to naturalise or fix political economy's laws in his reader's everyday experience. On the contrary, Marx's writing relies heavily on literary references, tropes, and genres in order to disturb political economy's theoretical equilibrium— training his readers to search for moments of abstract 'wretched evasions'.[41]

Even though he employs abstraction during his account of labour, Marx does not jump to Ricardo and Mill's 'aggregate sums', but dwells on labour *as a process*: 'Labour is the living, form-giving fire; it is the transitoriness of things, their temporality, as their formation by living time'.[42] A seemingly simple fire metaphor is used here, but it nonetheless offers a stark contrast with the earlier accumulative accounts of labour. *Living* time is spent in labour which is individualised and therefore humanised. When writing about 'money, or the circulation of commodities', Marx is careful to use bodily metaphors so as not to allow the naturalisation of money as divorced from labour to persist: 'Circulation sweats money from every pore'.[43] In animating and re-animating the labour process as living, Marx highlights again the gothic and vampiric nature of capital and capitalists:

> by incorporating living labour into their lifeless objectivity, the capitalist simultaneously transforms value, i.e. past labour in its objectified and lifeless form, into capital, value which can perform its own valorization process, an animated monster which begins to 'work', 'as if its body were by love possessed'.[44]

Finishing his critique with a reference to Goethe's tragic 1829 play, *Faust*, in which the main character makes a pact with a devil, Marx once again uses literary interventions to challenge the fixity of political economy's theories, asking his readers to read beyond a particular theory and instead read holistically.

Situating political economy within competing discourses, Marx's writing itself is animated and dynamic as he moves from mathematical depictions and abstractions to literary quotations. His readers must immerse themselves in the process of writing and theorising capital; they cannot only take the distant vantage point that calculation requires. Marx's writing style also despises neutrality in his assessment of political economists and their theories and therefore disrupts readerly and 'scientific' detachment from the subject matter, instead aiming to provoke and incite emotional reactions. Thus, of Mill he writes: 'On a level plain, simple mounds look like hills; and the insipid flatness of our present bourgeoisie is to be measured by the altitude of its "great intellects"'.[45] Scathing of his predecessors and their portrayal of the 'laws' of political economy, Marx instils distrust in his readers through the genres of writing he deploys and the secrets and puzzles he solves. Before he begins Part Six of Volume I: Wages, he concludes Part Five with

> Capital, therefore, is not only the command over labour, as Adam Smith thought. It is essentially the command over unpaid labour ... The secret of the self-valorization of capital resolves itself into the fact that it has at its disposal a definite quantity of the unpaid labour of other people.[46]

Having ended Part Five with a revelation, declaring a portion of people's labour as unpaid, he has simultaneously set the scene of mystery and tone of suspicion for the chapters to follow, challenging his readers to adopt his mode of scepticism. Marx's frequent juxtaposition of secrecy and revelation within his gothic style, therefore, codes classical political economy not only as requiring decipherment, but also as untrustworthy and potentially corrupting.

The Marginal and Mathematical Revolution

In the 1870s, political economy underwent a dramatic shift that would ensure it became even more entrenched as a science and harder to comprehend from outside its disciplinary boundaries; a shift that has come to be known as the Marginal Revolution, one that involved a mathematical revolution too. The narrative that our history of political economy has traced thus far (despite the differences between many of the political economists we have studied) has been centred on labour. But a new set of economic protagonists enter the story in the latter half of the nineteenth century: William Stanley Jevons, Alfred Marshall, Carl Menger, and Léon Walras. In a coincidence of history (working in England, Austria, and France, respectively), Jevons, Menger, and Walras would independently develop a marginal theory of utility and the principle of diminishing marginal utility—the theory that the satisfaction or utility gained from a product decreases incrementally with each additional unit of the product. These 'neoclassical' economists, as Thorstein Veblen would later dub them, thereby moved the centre of value analysis away from labour and production to that of utility and consumption. A profound change that would move the focus of study away from the *work* of the labourer to the *choices* of the consumer and therefore a new theory of value emerged that was concerned with human desires. This also signalled the shift from macroeconomic to microeconomic analyses, from Mill's 'national and universal results' to individual economic acts. As the extent of the similarities between Jevons', Menger's, and Walras' theories and their intellectual traditions, as well as the scale and novelty of the revolution has been widely debated, this section will focus on Jevons, or what the philosopher and economic historian Margaret Schabas has called a Jevonian revolution in England, and its legacies as well as its dissimilarities with Marshall's theories.[47] In his *Theory of Political Economy* (1871), Jevons eschews the labour theory of value, beginning not with labour (like Smith) or production (like Mill), but instead with the 'Mathematical Character of Science' arguing that 'value depends entirely upon utility' and that 'pleasure and pain are undoubtedly the ultimate objects of the Calculus of Economics'.[48] With this framing to his work Jevons strongly delimits the objectives of his *Theory* and his emphasis on calculus centres mathematics as the primary methodology of economics. In justifying his approach in his Preface, Jevons argues that as economics 'deals throughout with quantities, it must be a *mathematical science* in matter if not in language'.[49] Calculations are no longer a supplement to the theory, they are the very theory itself and the *language* by which that theory is explained. The difference between Smith and Jevons here appears absolute: no extrapolative analogies will suffice to demonstrate economic principles, its status as a science is inextricably linked to its reliance on mathematics: 'It is clear that Economics, if it is to be a science at all, must be a mathematical science'.[50]

And yet even within his insistence on economics' dependency on mathematics as a language of explanation, Jevons still relies on analogies to make his case:

> The Theory of Economy thus treated presents a close analogy to the science of Statical Mechanics . . . The nature of Wealth and Value is explained by the consideration of indefinitely small amounts of pleasure and pain, just as the Theory of Statics is made to rest upon the equality of indefinitely small amounts of energy.[51]

In trying to justify a unit of pleasure or pain as a measurable quantity, Jevons relies further on these analogies with the natural sciences, comparing the measurement of feelings to that of gravity's effects on a pendulum:

> We can no more know nor measure gravity in its own nature than we can measure a feeling; but, just as we measure gravity by its effects in the motion of a pendulum, so we may estimate the equality or inequality of feelings by the decisions of the human mind. The will is our pendulum, and its oscillations are minutely registered in the price lists of the markets.[52]

Despite arguing for the mathematical essence of economics, Jevons inadvertently demonstrates its limits as an explanatory language and instead highlights the necessity of imaginative narratives, asking his readers to imagine the significance of mathematical economics through the comparison with other sciences and invoking metaphors of measurement.

Jevons' argument for the 'mathematical character of economics' is not simply about making a case for the explanatory and methodological tools necessary for economics to be treated as a science but about divorcing economics from its historical adjective—political—with all its social and ethical baggage. In categorising economics relations with the 'hierarchy of feeling', Jevons is clear that economics deals with the 'lowest rank of feelings' (i.e. pleasure and pain').[53] This curtailing of the moral imperative traceable in the work of Smith is key. Economics is not concerned with the domain of ethics, according to Jevons:

> Each labourer, in the absence of other motives, is supposed to devote his energy to the accumulation of wealth. A higher calculus of moral right and wrong would be needed to show how he may best employ that wealth for the good of others as well as himself.[54]

It must be noted here that Jevons is not claiming that there is no role for ethics to play in society—indeed Jevons considers his theory in relation to Jeremy Bentham's moral theory of Utilitarianism—but that ethical questions are not the domain of economics, which should remain a mathematical science. The significance of the trust placed in mathematical calculations and the separation of 'economics' from the ethical dimensions and social questions evoked by 'political' cannot be overstated: it would have enormous influence on the development of neoliberal economics in the twentieth century and the faith in the competitive market embraced by the work of Friedrich Hayek and Milton Friedman.

Notwithstanding his reliance on analogies, Jevons' designation of mathematics as the language of economics seems to position literature and narrative as impossibly distant from the concerns of economics. Yet literary scholars have made a strong case for the shared interests of writers and artists of the late nineteenth century, particularly *fin de siècle* writers, who participated in the aesthetic and decadent movements (such as Oscar Wilde, Henry James, and Walter Pater) and the economic theories of the neoclassical school of economics.[55] The economic shift to a focus on human desires and consumerism, meant that economic value came to be more individualised, subjective, and psychological than the previous focus on macroeconomic labour and production allowed. Consider, too, the individualised and subjective focus on character's desire in texts like *The Picture of Dorian Gray* (1890) or *The Spoils of Poynton* (1897), where consumption is portrayed as both intimate and all-consuming. Although ironically summarised by James' 'Preface' as a 'story of cabinets and chairs and tables', *The Spoils of Poynton* also burns with an insatiable desire best expressed by Fleda Vetch when she learns that all of Poynton's precious possessions have been lost in the fire:

> Mixed with the horror, with the kindness of the station-master, with the smell of cinders and the riot of sound was the raw bitterness of a hope that she might never again in life have to give up so much at such short notice.[56]

Mathematical economics and literary aesthetics can still, therefore, intersect in their studies of human desires and consumption.

A contemporary of Jevons, founder of the Cambridge School of Economics, and one of the most influential economists at the turn of the century, Alfred Marshall was also a consummate mathematician, having studied mathematics before he became an economist. Yet Marshall's view of the relationship between economics and mathematics was (while also not consistent over his long career) different from Jevons. Marshall cautioned against the too frequent application of mathematics to economics as he was concerned that economics would become too abstract and divorced from the real world and real economic actors. He made a distinction between 'mathematical language' and 'mathematical habits of thought' arguing in an apparent jab at Jevons that it is 'doubtful whether much has been gained by the use of complex mathematical formulae' whereas the 'application of mathematical habits of thought has been of great service'.[57] In a famous 1906 letter to one of his previous students, Arthur Lyon Bowley, he wrote that the use of mathematics should be limited and be used only 'as a shorthand language rather than an engine of inquiry' and advised to 'burn the mathematics'.[58] In other words, mathematics should supplement, rather than replace, political economy. Though Marshall acknowledged the significance of abstraction to economics, he was also concerned with economics having real world applicability. In stark contrast with Jevons' focus on the mathematical character, the opening chapters of Marshall's *Principles of Economics* (1890) instead outline economics as 'as study of mankind in the ordinary business of life', but one that must acknowledge that, in business, people are still influenced by 'personal affections', 'conceptions of duty', and 'reverence for high ideals'.[59] Economic actors are therefore complex, and the 'pursuit of abstractions is a good thing, when confined to its proper place', but economics needs to be 'in touch with the actual conditions of life'.[60]

The scope Marshall provides for economics in his *Principles* is therefore broad, being the

> study of the economic aspects and conditions of man's political, social and private life; but more especially of his social life. The aims of the study are to gain knowledge for its own sake, and to obtain guidance in the practical conduct of life, and especially of social life.[61]

He critiques Ricardo and his supporters for 'regard[ing] man as a constant quantity' and 'never [giving] themselves enough trouble to study his variations'.[62] Marshall's background in ethics undoubtedly also shaped his views about the role economics should play in theorising human behaviour. He recalls how after reading Mill he had 'doubts about the propriety of inequality of *opportunity*' and how during his vacations he 'visited the poorest quarters of several cities and walked through one street after another, looking at the faces of the poorest people. Next, I resolved to make as thorough a study as I could of Political Economy'.[63] In his appendix he complains that Mill's commitment to considering political economy in *relation* to social philosophy is too frequently ignored, and 'it is forgotten that his treatment of economic questions took constant account of many motives besides the desire for wealth'.[64] Importantly, Marshall was resituating ethical concerns within economics. The impact ethics was allowed to have on economics remained limited, but Marshall was returning to the foundations of political economy to reassert the moral and social implications of economic theory. As his most famous student, John Maynard Keynes recorded: 'It was only through Ethics that he first reached Economics'.[65]

That Marshall wanted economics to be a dynamic science responsive to everyday life rather than a static theory, is evident from his definition of equilibrium, which he describes in his most famous metaphor as a pair of scissors:

'We might as reasonably dispute whether it is the upper or the under blade of a pair of scissors that cuts a piece of paper, as whether value is governed by utility or cost of production'. Warning against 'careless brevity', Marshall argues for the importance of 'strictly scientific' accounts in contrast to 'merely popular' claims.[66] A grand explanatory narrative of microeconomics (in the vein of Smith's macroeconomic invisible hand), Marshall's theory of equilibrium is nonetheless subject to, and complicated by, the impact of time. Taking account of the real world, Marshall re-evaluates the concept of static equilibrium, clarifying that

> in real life such oscillations are seldom as rhythmical as those of a stone hanging freely from a string; the comparison would be more exact if the string were supposed to hang in the troubled waters of a mill-race, whose stream was at one time allowed to flow freely, and at another partially cut off.[67]

Not only is Marshall attempting to theorise an economics drawn from the real world, but he is also using literary tools with which to explicate his theory. Although he disparagingly contrasts economic 'facts' with poetic 'ideals' in the *Principles*, Marshall relies heavily on metaphors such as the scissors or the stone on the string to explain complex economic theories such as equilibrium or the price elasticity of demand. These metaphors and analogies conjure up imaginative comparisons that counterintuitively allow Marshall to ground his theory in the real world. In the same way that Smith used everyday objects to explain the labour theory of value, Marshall's quotidian analogies help his readers understand the applicability and the necessary adaptability of his theories. Economics is concerned with ordinary yet changeable daily life. Marshall's metaphoric explanations and worlded analogies would have a profound influence on the economist who would dominate the first half of the twentieth century: John Maynard Keynes.

The Middle Way

An economist as well as an adept historian of economic thought, Keynes was deeply attuned to the fragility of economics as an explanatory and predictive discourse of human desires and behaviour. Building on Marshall's theorising of time, marginal efficiency, and the social life of economic actors, Keynes criticised past economic theories for relying on idealised static versions of the economy and human behaviour, what he called the 'special case' of classical economy. In *A Tract on Monetary Reform* (1923), Keynes returns us to Marshall's 'troubled waters' metaphor, famously sallying:

> The *long run* is a misleading guide to current affairs. *In the long run* we are all dead. Economists set themselves too easy, too useless a task, if in

tempestuous seasons they can only tell us that when the storm is long past the ocean is flat again.[68]

Keynes was even more damning of the Ricardian influence on economic theory than Marshall, decrying the individualist utopianism he found in Ricardo's works. Puzzled by the 'completeness of the Ricardian victory', he sarcastically argued that its 'intellectual prestige' derived from the unexpectedness of its conclusions:

That its teaching, translated into practice, was austere and often unpalatable, lent it virtue. That it was adapted to carry a vast and consistent logical superstructure, gave it beauty. That it could explain much social injustice and apparent cruelty as an inevitable incident in the scheme of progress, and the whole to do more harm than good, commanded it to authority. That it afforded a measure of justification to the free activities of the individualist capitalist, attracted to it the support of the dominant social force behind authority.[69]

In response, Keynes set himself the task of carving what came to be known as the 'middle way' in economic theory: the attempt to bridge the gap between unchecked individualism and complete governmental control of the economy. A critic of rampant individualism and classical economy's faith in the rationality of the individual, Keynes nonetheless strongly supported the 'liberty of the individual' arguing that if individualism could be 'purged of its defects and its abuses' it remained the 'best safeguard of personal liberty' and 'the best safeguard of the variety of life, which emerges precisely from this extended field of personal choice, and the loss of which is the greatest of all the losses of the homogenous or totalitarian state'.[70] Keynes' 'middle way' instead aimed to hold economics accountable for its failures and limitations as a theory by not allowing for poverty, inequalities, or depressions to simply be dismissed as the excusable results of individual actions.

Resembling 'Euclidean geometers in a non-Euclidean world', Keynes ridiculed economists for being too vulnerable to the seduction of beautiful mathematical formulas: 'discovering that in experience straight lines apparently parallel often meet, [classical economists] rebuke the lines for not keeping straight as the only remedy for the unfortunate collisions which are occurring'.[71] In contrast, Keynes acknowledged that human nature was subject to 'animal spirits' and 'spontaneous optimism' that could not necessarily be explained by 'mathematical expectations' or the 'outcome of a weighted average of quantitative benefits multiplied by quantitative probabilities'.[72] Yet, as Matt Seybold has argued, one of the central ironies of Keynes' heavy critique of the classical economic utopianism of a market balanced by individual actions is that in attempting to save economics from what he saw as the damaging Ricardian legacy, he, too, worked 'toward[s] his own utopian ends'. The very title of his magnum opus, *The General Theory of Employment, Interest, and Money* (1936), suggests that Keynes was attempting to write 'an audacious political economy designed to save the world from an audacious political economy'.[73] Keynes strongly believed in the concept and ability of what he called the 'master-economist': 'He must understand symbols and speak in words. He must contemplate the particular in terms of the general, and touch abstract and concrete in the same flight of thought'.[74] The modernist writer, Virginia Woolf, captured this idealist spirit in her unpublished biographical fragment 'JMK', which is undoubtedly a reference to Keynes. She imagines JMK committing himself to a

> great green board on which were pinned sheets of symbols: a frolic of xs controlled by ys and embraced by more cryptic symbols still: which if juggled together would eventually, he was sure, positive, produce the one word, the simple, the sufficient, the comprehensive word which will solve all problems forever. It was time to begin. He began.[75]

The utopianism of the one, 'comprehensive', heroic word that would resolve the world's problems is matched by Keynes' commitment to a *general* theory that he believed *could* unite individual liberty with a reconstituted economy that took account of the 'arbitrary and inequitable distribution of wealth and incomes' and allowed for government intervention to correct market failures.[76]

Woolf's admiration of Keynes' writing also reveals the stylistic consciousness of his economic writing. Keynes argued that the master economist needed to be 'mathematician, historian, statesman, philosopher', and his personal and professional writings reveal his strong commitment to studying the history of political economy, including its styles and genres. He wrote of Malthus, for example that he was always trying and failing to write 'big books' because he 'lacked the power of rapid executing and continuous concentration'. In Smith he detected a 'continuous artistic sensibility' which gave him alone 'the glory of the Quarto'. Other economists 'must pluck the day, fling pamphlets into the wind, write always *sub specie temporis*, and achieve immortality by accident, if at all'.[77] While Keynes criticised some economists for their mathematical aestheticisation of economics, there is no doubt that he deployed his own forms of aestheticisation, frequently using witty metaphors, aphorisms, and carefully balanced paradoxes and reversals to dismiss theories he disagreed with. In questioning the rhetoric of security and stability deployed in promising investment discourse, Keynes, for example, writes:

> Enterprise only pretends to itself to be mainly actuated by the statements in its own prospectus, however candid and sincere. Only a little more than an expedition to the South Pole, is it based on an exact calculation of benefits to come.[78]

Summarising his approach in the preface to his *General Theory*, Keynes wrote: 'The difficulty lies, not in the new ideas, but in escaping from the old ones, which ramify, for those brought up as most of us have been, into every corner of our minds'.[79] With faint echoes of Mill's claim that the 'only difficulty' remaining in political economy is to explain pre-existing theories and laws, Keynes reverses this assertion, arguing that it is exactly the weight and historic stability of these economic foundations that is the problem he aims to correct.

The Neoliberal Victory

If Keynes saw his economic predecessors as dominated by the Ricardian victory, then his successors would be defined by a neoliberal victory and the ascendency of the theories of Austrian economist, Friedrich Hayek, and their further development by the American economist, Milton Friedman. A reaction to fascist Germany, Franklin D. Roosevelt's New Deal, the postwar settlement, and the rising socialist rhetoric he encountered in his adoptive Britain, Hayek's most famous book, *The Road to Serfdom* (1944) warned against what he saw as the dangerous increase in anti-capitalist sentiment and the 'death of capitalism' discourse pervading British intellectual society. Hayek cautioned that government intervention in the economy would lead to fascism, revealing the 'unpalatable truth that it is Germany whose fate we are in some danger of repeating'. Hayek was damning of Keynes' 'middle way' approach to economics, arguing that it was this very approach that naively led society down the road to serfdom: 'If we are nevertheless rapidly moving towards such a [centralised] state this is largely because most people still believe that it must be possible to find some Middle Way between "atomistic" competition and central direction'. While 'competition can bear some admixture of regulation', Hayek is adamant that 'it cannot be combined with planning to any extent we like without ceasing to operate as an effective guide to production'.[80]

Hayek is advocating for the economic market as the best adjudicator of economic *and* social decisions, arguing that 'we do not possess moral standards that enable us to settle' questions of equality and justice 'to a greater general satisfaction than is done by the competitive market'.[81] Inequality is perfectly justifiable and certainly no reason to intervene in the market, Hayek claims, arguing in *Individualism and the Economic Order* (1958): 'that only because men are in fact unequal can we treat them equally. If all men were completely equal in their gifts and inclinations, we should have to treat them differently in order to achieve any sort of social organisation'.[82] Because they are fallible, human beings cannot be relied on to organise society in a better or more efficient way than the market. There are clear echoes here of Smith's celebration of the metaphoric invisible hand of the market that efficiently 'distributes the necessaries of life' and 'advance[s] the interests of society'. It is this commitment to the spontaneous order achieved by the market, despite its resultant inequalities that 'gets at the crux of the conflict' between the ideals of neoliberalism and those of social democracy, according to the economic historian Gareth Stedman Jones. For Hayek, his Mont Pelerin Society colleagues, and his followers, social freedom and individual liberty were dependent on economic freedom. The uninterrupted, competitive market, therefore, becomes the ultimate symbol of freedom—a negative liberty which guarantees the lack of intervention, rather than the positive freedom sought by socialist democrats striving for a more egalitarian society.[83]

Yet despite the celebration of the competitive market for its amorality—and thereby, the neoliberal theory he outlines—Hayek codes *The Road to Serfdom* and his economic approach as a moral account, stating clearly in his preface that the writing of this book 'is a duty [he] cannot evade'.[84] And though they were intellectual and economic rivalries, Keynes recognised and responded favourably to the moral and philosophical underpinnings of Hayek's work. Writing to Hayek in 1944 that 'morally and philosophically I find myself in agreement with virtually the whole of it; and not only agreement with it, but in deeply moved agreement', Keynes acknowledged that '[w]e all have the greatest reason to be grateful to you for saying so well what needs so much to be said'.[85] Keynes' language here mirrors Hayek's appeals to duty and the sense of a social moral crisis that he needs to correct through his celebration of the market and individualism. The 'correction' to liberalism undertaken by Hayek would resonate globally and have profound political implications. Beginning with Winston Churchill (who disastrously used the themes of Hayek's *Road* in an attempt to discredit Clement Atlee's Labour Party's socialism as a form of nascent fascism in 1945), Hayek's commitment to protecting the individual's independent relation to the market has been instrumental in shaping the ideological foundations of Margaret Thatcher—'there is no such thing as society'—and Ronald Reagan, as well as ushering in neoliberalism as the governing social and political philosophy of contemporary society. Following the Thatcher-Reaganite era, neoliberalism would become a 'hegemonic discourse' that, according to Marxist geographer David Harvey, 'has become incorporated into the common-sense way many of us interpret, live in, and understand the world' and led to the mass privatisation of what had previously been seen as public services and goods: the commons.[86]

The political intent of neoliberalism as developed by Hayek's economic and ideological successor, Milton Friedman, is clear from the opening passage of his *Capitalism and Freedom* (1962) which pitches the neoliberal economic philosophy against the spirit of political duty proposed by John F. Kennedy's famous question in his inaugural address: 'ask not what your country can do for you, but what you can do for your country'. Friedman dismisses the question as at once paternalistic, organismic, and opposed to true conceptions of freedom: 'To the free man, the country is the collection of individuals who compose it, not something over and above them'.[87] Adamant that the major crisis facing contemporary society's freedom is the 'concentration of power' and arguing that the 'scope of government must be limited', Friedman further

Courting the Imagination 27

cements the social and political agenda of neoliberalism in his first chapter, 'the relation between economic freedom and political freedom'.[88] In organising the argument of his book, Friedman strategically limits the capacity of government by confining the thematic weight he gives it:

> [The book's] major theme is the role of competitive capitalism—the organization of the bulk of economic activity through private enterprise operating in a free market—as a system of economic freedom and a necessary condition for political freedom. Its minor theme is the role that government should play in a society dedicated to freedom and relying primarily on the market to organize economic activity.[89]

Friedman's conceptualisation of 'political' is not, however, the same sense of the political we encountered in the theories of the eighteenth and nineteenth centuries when the 'political' attached to *political* economy was as seen as a way to counteract the excesses of the market that allowed for government intervention to correct market 'failures'. Friedman's understanding of the economy as political is, rather, the process by which the market replaces the political and social counterweights to the economy because, by his reckoning, the market is the most 'just' adjudicator of human affairs.

Not only is the competitive market the best regulator of human activity because it 'permits unanimity without conformity', Friedman argues that government intervention stifles economic progress and leads to creative stagnation.[90] Unlike Hayek, Friedman believed that even private monopolies were preferable to government intervention, and he therefore argued for the radical limitation of governmental roles, insisting on the privatisation of social security, charity, aged care, and even education, committing himself to a lifelong campaign for the school vouchers programme.[91] Aware that his claims for the market as the most appealing organiser of society and as the most practical barrier to monopoly formation may strike many as, at best, exaggerated and, at worst, implausible, Friedman makes an ironic appeal to the Euclidean simile Keynes had so deftly deployed against utopian market proselytisers previously:

> Of course, competition is an ideal type, like a Euclidean line or point. No one has ever seen a Euclidean line—which has zero width and depth—yet we all find it useful to regard many a Euclidean volume—such as a surveyor's string—as a Euclidean line. Similarly, there is no such thing as 'pure' competition.[92]

This is a return to the abstraction of the economy from real world circumstances (though Friedman would argue otherwise), and it is therefore not surprising that in attempting to rebrand liberalism, *Capitalism and Freedom* is marked by a political and economic nostalgia with frequent appeals to what

Friedman terms the radical liberalism of the nineteenth century: 'the intellectual movement that went under the name of liberalism emphasized freedom as the ultimate goal and the individual as the ultimate entity in the society'. In celebrating *laissez-faire* economics, 'the nineteenth-century liberal regarded an extension of freedom as the most effective way to promote welfare and equality', in contrast to the 'twentieth-century liberal [who] regards welfare and equality as either prerequisites of or an alternative to freedom'.[93] With the reliance on the market to regulate society, Friedman again returns us to Smith's invisible hand (which he explicitly cites in the book). This return to Smith is interesting as it is a reconstructed Smith; a version of Smith created in the image of the neoliberal market evangeliser, and it is therefore fitting that Friedman relies on *this* Smith to close his narrative of market utopianism:

> As Adam Smith once said, 'There is much ruin in a nation'. . . I believe that we shall be able to preserve and extend freedom . . . only if we awake to the threat we face, only if we persuade our fellow men that free institutions offer a surer, if perhaps at times a slower, route to the ends they seek than the coercive power of the state.

Observing a 'glimmering of change' in his 'intellectual climate', Friedman categorised them as a 'hopeful augury' of his grand narrative of economic and political liberty which could only be guaranteed by the free market.[94]

Notes

1 Recognising the success of Smith in making these economic ideas popular is not to deny the significance of his influences. See, for example, Albert O. Hirschman, *The Passions and the Interests* (Princeton: Princeton University Press, 1977); Emma Rothschild, *Economic Sentiments: Adam Smith, Condorcet, and the Enlightenment* (Cambridge, MA: Harvard University Press, 2001).
2 See, for example, Vivienne Brown, *Adam Smith's Discourse: Canonicity, Commerce and Conscience* (London and New York: Routledge, 1994).
3 Adam Smith, *The Wealth of Nations: Complete and Unabridged*, ed. Edwin Cannan and intro. Robert Reich (New York: Random House, 2000), I.I, 4.
4 Smith, *Wealth of Nations*, I.I, 4, 5.
5 The Smith £20 note was replaced by the artist J. M. W. Turner in 2020.
6 Adam Smith, 'History of Astronomy', in *The Glasgow Edition of the Works and Correspondence of Adam Smith: III: Essays on Philosophical Subjects: With Dugal Stewart's "Account of Adam Smith"*, ed. J. C. Bryce and William P. D. Wightman (Oxford: Oxford University Press, 1980), IV, 32–33.
7 Smith, *Wealth of Nations*, I.I, 12.
8 Smith, *Wealth of Nations*, I.I, 12.

9 Smith, *Wealth of Nations*, I.II, 14.
10 Smith, *Wealth of Nations*, IV.II, 485.
11 Adam Smith, *The Theory of Moral Sentiments and on the Origins of Languages*, ed. Dugald Stewart (Henry G. Bohn, 1853), IV.I, 263–265.
12 Deirdre McCloskey, *If You're so Smart: The Narrative of Economic Expertise* (Chicago: Chicago University Press, 1990), 1.
13 Adam Smith, *Lectures on Jurisprudence*, ed. R. L. Meel, D. D. Raphael, and P. G. Stein (Oxford: Oxford University Press, 1978), 397.
14 Smith, *Wealth of Nations*, IV, 455.
15 David Ricardo, *The Works and Correspondence of David Ricardo: I: On the Principles of Political Economy and Taxation*, ed. Piero Sraffa and M. H. Dobb (Cambridge: Cambridge University Press, 1951), 5.
16 Smith, *Wealth of Nations*, I, 455.
17 Ricardo, *The Works and Correspondence of David Ricardo*, 25.
18 For a longer discussion of Smith's woollen coat and the differences with Ricardo's abstraction, see Sarah Comyn, *Political Economy and the Novel: A Literary History of "Homo Economicus"* (Basingstoke: Palgrave Macmillan, 2018).
19 Charles Dickens, 'On Strike', *Household Words* VIII, no. 203 (February 1854), 558.
20 Robert Torrens, *An Essay on the Production of Wealth; with an Appendix in Which the Principles of Political Economy are Applied to the Actual Circumstances of the Country* (London: Longman, Hurst, Rees, Orme and Brown, 1821), iv.
21 See, for example, Claudia C. Klaver, *A/Moral Economics: Classical Political Economy and Cultural Authority in Nineteenth-Century England* (Columbus: Ohio State University Press, 2003); Mary Poovey, *Genres of the Credit Economy: Mediating Value in Eighteenth- and Nineteenth-Century Britain* (Chicago: University of Chicago Press, 2008).
22 Jane Marcet, *Conversations on Political Economy; in Which the Elements of that Science are Familiarly Explained*, 6th ed. revised and enlarged (London: Longman, Rees, Orme, Brown and Green, 1827), vi.
23 Jane Marcet, *Conversations on Political Economy; in Which the Elements of that Science are Familiarly Explained* (London: Longman, Rees, Orme, Brown and Green, 1816), 18.
24 Jane Marcet, *Conversations on Political Economy; in Which the Elements of that Science are Familiarly Explained*, 2nd ed. (London: Longman, Rees, Orme, Brown and Green, 1817), 18.
25 Marcet, *Conversations* (1816), 13.
26 John Stuart Mill, *Autobiography of John Stuart Mill* (Auckland: The Floating Press, 2009), 31.
27 John Stuart Mill, *Principles of Political Economy with Some of Their Applications to Social Philosophy*, ed. and intro. William James Ashley, 7th ed. (London: Longmans, Green and Co., 1923), 1, III.I, 437; John Stuart Mill, *Essays on Some Unsettled Questions of Political Economy*, 3rd ed. (London: Londmans, Green and Co., 1877), 137–138.

28 Mill, *Principles*, I.II, 29–30.
29 Mill, *Principles*, I.II, 30.
30 Mill, *Principles*, I.II, 42.
31 John Kells Ingram, *A History of Political Economy* (Edinburgh: Adam and Charles Black, 1888), 224. See, also, Joseph Persky, 'Retrospectives: the Ethology of Homo Economicus', *Journal of Economic Perspectives* 2 (1994), 221–231.
32 Mill, *Principles*, III.I, 438.
33 Mill, *Principles*, III.I, 436.
34 Mill, *Autobiography*, 148.
35 Karl Marx, *Capital: Volume 1*, intro. Ernest Mandel and trans. Ben Fowkes (London and New York: Penguin Classics, 1990), 643.
36 Marx, *Capital*, 653.
37 Marx, *Capital*, 163–164.
38 Marx, *Capital*, 149.
39 For more on Marx's gothic economies see, for example, Gail Turley Houston, *From Dickens to Dracula: Gothic, Economics, and Victorian Fiction* (Cambridge: Cambridge University Press, 2005).
40 Marx, *Capital*, 167.
41 Marx, *Capital*, 652.
42 Karl Marx, *Grundrisse: Foundations of the Critique of Political Economy (Rough Draft)*, trans. Martin Nicolaus (London: Allen Lane, 1973), 361.
43 Marx, *Capital*, 208.
44 Marx, *Capital*, 302.
45 Marx, *Capital*, 654.
46 Marx, *Capital*, 672.
47 Margaret Schabas, 'Alfred Marshall, W. Stanley Jevons, and the Mathematization of Economics', *Isis* 80, no. 1 (1989), 60–73 (60–61).
48 W. Stanley Jevons, *Theory of Political Economy*, 2nd ed. revised and enlarged (London: Macmillan and Co., 1879), 1–3, 40.
49 Jevons, *Theory of Political Economy*, vii.
50 Jevons, *Theory of Political Economy*, 3.
51 Jevons, *Theory of Political Economy*, vii.
52 Jevons, *Theory of Political Economy*, 13.
53 Jevons, *Theory of Political Economy*, 29.
54 Jevons, *Theory of Political Economy*, 29.
55 See, for example, Regenia Gagnier, *The Insatiability of Human Wants: Economics and Aesthetics in Market Society* (Chicago: University of Chicago Press, 2000).
56 Henry James, *The Spoils of Poynton*, ed. Bernard Richards (Oxford: Oxford World Classics, 2008), xvi, 184.
57 Alfred Marshall, *Principles of Economics*, 8th ed. (London: Macmillan and Co., Ltd., 1949), 71.
58 Alfred Marshall to A. Bowley, 27 February 1906, in *Memorials of Alfred Marshall*, ed. A. C. Pigou (London: Macmillan, 1925; rpt., New York: Augustus M. Kelly, 1966), 427.
59 Marshall, *Principles*, 1, 12.

60 Marshall, *Principles*, 645.
61 Marshall, *Principles*, 35.
62 Marshall, *Principles*, 630.
63 Recorded by John Maynard Keynes, 'Alfred Marshall, 1842–1924', *The Economic Journal* 34, no. 135 (1924), 311–372 (319).
64 Marshall, *Principles*, 645.
65 Keynes, 'Alfred Marshall', 319.
66 Marshall, *Principles*, 290.
67 Marshall, *Principles*, 288.
68 John Maynard Keynes, *A Tract on Monetary Reform* (London: Macmillan, 1923), 80 (emphasis in original).
69 John Maynard Keynes, *The General Theory of Employment, Interest, and Money*, intro. Paul Krugman (London: Macmillan for the Royal Economic Society, 2007), 32–33.
70 Keynes, *The General Theory*, 380.
71 Keynes, *The General Theory*, 16.
72 Keynes, *The General Theory*, 161.
73 Matt Seybold, 'The End of Economics', *Los Angeles Review of Books*, 3 July 2017, https://lareviewofbooks.org/article/the-end-of-economics/
74 Keynes, 'Alfred Marshall', 322.
75 Virginia Woolf, 'John Maynard Keynes by Virginia Woolf', in *The Bloomsbury Group: A Collection of Memoirs and Commentary*, ed. S. P. Rosenbaum, revised ed. (Toronto: Toronto University Press, 1995), 275. For a longer discussion of the aesthetic relationship between Woolf and Keynes, see Comyn, *Political Economy and the Novel*, 133–172.
76 Keynes, *The General Theory*, 372.
77 Keynes, 'Alfred Marshall', 343–344.
78 Keynes, *The General Theory*, 162.
79 Keynes, *The General Theory*, viii.
80 Friedrich von Hayek, *The Road to Serfdom* (London: Routledge, 2007), 43.
81 Hayek, *Road to Serfdom*, 35.
82 Friedrich von Hayek, *Individualism and the Economic Order* (Chicago: University of Chicago Press, 1958), 15–16.
83 Gareth Stedman Jones, *Masters of the Universe: Hayek, Friedman, and the Birth of Neoliberal Politics* (Princeton: Princeton University Press, 2012), 63–70.
84 Hayek, *Road to Serfdom*, v.
85 J. M. Keynes to Friedrich von Hayek, 28 June 1944, cited in Comyn, *Political Economy and the Novel*, 194.
86 David Harvey, 'Neoliberalism as Creative Destruction', *The Annals of the American Academy of Political and Social Science* 610 (2007), 22–44, http://www.jstor.org/stable/25097888
87 Milton Friedman, *Capitalism and Freedom* (Chicago: University of Chicago Press, 2002), 1–2.
88 Friedman, *Capitalism and Freedom*, 2, 7.
89 Friedman, *Capitalism and Freedom*, 4.

90 Friedman, *Capitalism and Freedom*, 23.
91 Friedman, *Capitalism and Freedom*, 20.
92 Friedman, *Capitalism and Freedom*, 120.
93 Friedman, *Capitalism and Freedom*, 5.
94 Friedman, *Capitalism and Freedom*, 202.

2 Grand Economic Narratives

Homo Economicus

The primary agent of economic theory, *homo economicus* or economic man, is also one of its foundational grand narratives; traceable to the liberal individual of the eighteenth century and Adam Smith's *Wealth of Nations*. In proposing the 'invisible hand of the market', Smith also suggests *homo economicus*' two defining characteristics: rational self-interest. Every economic individual, according to Smith, is 'continually exerting himself to find out the most advantageous employment for whatever capital he can command'. He seeks 'his own advantage' and 'not that of the society', but 'the study of his own advantage naturally, or rather necessarily, leads him to prefer that employment which is most advantageous to the society'.[1] While the self-interest is explicit, the rationality is implied through its attachment to self-interested behaviour. Smith writes of this self-interested pursuit of economic wealth as perfectly rational and natural: 'it is only for the sake of profit that any man employs a capital in the support of industry; and he will always, therefore, endeavour to employ it' to achieve 'the greatest quantity either of money or of other goods'. The 'he will always, *therefore*' achieves the logical alignment between naturalised self-interest and rational behaviour. Indeed, according to Smith, pursuing the 'public good' through economic actions is *irrational* behaviour that needs to be dissuaded: 'I have never known much good done by those who affected to trade for the public good. It is an affectation, indeed, not very common among merchants, and very few words need be employed in dissuading them from it'.[2]

Although Smith writes a normative account here of economic behaviour that supports a *laissez-faire* approach to the market, this is not to say he thought men were infallible or always rational. Smith was keenly aware of and anxious about potentially irrational passions and drives—'avarice and ambition in the rich' and the 'hatred of labour and the love of present ease and enjoyment' in the poor—that humans could succumb to and attempted to find means of regulating them. It was also in response to property (especially, newly mobile property) that Smith thought the irrational passions could easily be excited and the need for civil government arose, arguing that '[w]here there is no property, or at least none that exceeds the value of two or three days labour, civil government is not so necessary'.[3] The governing power of prudence, however, performed a counteraction and moderation to these impulses for Smith. In combination with this theory of jurisprudence (in which justice as the 'foundation of civil government' was one of his four pillars), Smith created a 'moral social vision' in which the market economy could operate. Like the balancing and guiding action of the invisible hand, 'the principles of common prudence . . . always influence that of the majority of every class or order'.[4] The generalised appeal to a common behaviour or rationality is therefore codified and protects against potentially damaging passions:

> It can seldom happen, indeed, that the circumstances of a great nation can be much affected either by the prodigality or misconduct of individuals; the profusion or imprudence of some being always more than compensated by the frugality and good conduct of others.[5]

While for Smith and Ricardo, the rationality was implied, for Mill, to whom the invention of *homo economicus* was credited, the rationality was explicit. As we have seen in the previous chapter, Mill was adamant about the use of abstractions in political economy and frequently emphasised the *scientific* foundations of his approach: 'in considering exchange value scientifically'; 'those who are accustomed to any kind of scientific investigation'; 'in scientific discussion'; 'I regard it as proved, both scientifically and historically', etc.[6] This was crucial to the delineation of political economy as a scientific discipline, but it also highlighted rationality as one of the defining characteristics of Mill's model of the economic actor. In his discussion of the minimum rate of profit, Mill argued that an 'industrial life exercises' influence 'over the passions and inclinations of human nature' that leads to an increase in providence and supports and is, in turn, supported by rational behaviour:

> In proportion as life has fewer vicissitudes, as habits become more fixed, and great prizes are less and less to be hoped for by any other means than long perseverance, mankind become more willing to sacrifice present indulgence for future objects. This increased capacity of forethought and self-control may assuredly find other things to exercise itself upon than increase of riches.[7]

By contrast, as we have seen in the last chapter, Keynes (and his intellectual ancestor, Marshall) was, following Smith, concerned by the human propensity to be driven by irrational 'passions and inclinations', what Keynes termed 'animal spirits'. In his diagnosis of the stock market, Keynes' ridiculed economists' faith in the rationality of the economic actor arguing that '[i]n estimating the prospects of investment, we must have regard, therefore, to the nerves and hysteria and even the digestions and reactions to the weather of those upon whose spontaneous activity it largely depends'. Keynes was not suggesting that 'everything depends on waves of irrational psychology', acknowledging that the 'state of long-term expectation is often steady'. Instead, Keynes was reminding his readers that 'human decisions affecting the future, whether personal or political or economic, cannot depend on strict mathematical expectation, since the basis for making such calculations does not exist'. Even though our 'rational selves' try to choose 'between the alternatives as best we are able', we often fall back 'for our motive on whim or sentiment or chance'.[8]

Economic man *seems* to be given the greatest endorsement by neoliberal theories of the market, but Hayek was in fact very sceptical about overstating the rationality of the individual. He critiqued Mill's faith in the rational individual and believed it played a crucial role in eroding classical liberalism. Hayek attacked the uncritical trust in *homo economicus* because it gave people a false sense of security: believing that adjustments or interventions in the market could be benevolent. Rather, for Hayek, it was only the self-adjusting market that should be trusted. The most celebratory account of *homo economicus* is to be found, not in economic theories, but instead in the infamous 1957 novel by Ayn Rand: *Atlas Shrugged*. In the book, rationality and self-interest are seen as the primary engines of a prosperous and creative society. The hero of Rand's novel, John Galt, claims that 'there is no conflict of interests among men, neither in business nor in trade nor in their most personal desires—if they omit the irrational from their view of the possible and destruction from their view of the practical'.[9] Any form of market intervention is seen as evil, and those who cannot keep up with the successful economic men are considered weak and unworthy of assistance or even consideration. The American writer and critic, Gore Vidal, characterised Rand's philosophy as 'nearly perfect in its immorality', while the conservative journalist, Whittaker Chambers wrote in a scathing review that 'From almost every page of *Atlas Shrugged*, a voice can be heard, from painful necessity, commanding: "To a gas chamber—go!"'.[10] Yet Rand's work had a powerful influence on the political and economic landscape of the United States of America. Included among her acolytes are President Ronald Reagan; former Speaker of the House and Tea Party supporter, Paul Ryan; and former Chairman of the Federal Reserve, Alan Greenspan. Greenspan served as Chairman for five terms from 1987 to 2005—an extraordinary long term with profound implications for the United States' fiscal policy and for global economics.[11]

Despite the shaky foundations evident in this grand narrative, however, *homo economicus* has had a surprising longevity and has persistently been able to cleave to economic models and shape financial policies. Gary Becker's influential work applied the logic of cost-benefit analysis to racial discrimination, criminality, education, and even family dynamics, arguing for the significance of investing in *human capital* or the 'resources *in* people' that influence their 'future monetary and psychic income'.[12] The extension of the traits of rationality and self-interest to calculations beyond the economic realm is clear in the economic-language creep of psychic income and resources. Yet feminist economists have long noted the one-dimensionality and androcentrism of *homo economicus*. With its acronym, as Susan F. Feiner has adroitly noted, of 'he', the characteristics of 'economic actors map (too perfectly to be coincidental) onto traditional notions of masculinity', and 'as subjects' in the history of economics, women have 'largely been absent'.[13] Women have been, however, key players, both in crucial economic events historically *and*, as has already been shown in the previous chapter, in developing political economy not simply as a scientific discipline but one with a wide and growing audience. So much so that in an 1822 letter to her aunt, Mrs Ruxton, the Anglo-Irish novelist, Maria Edgeworth sardonically exclaimed that it 'has now become high fashion with blue ladies to talk Political Economy' and make 'a great jabbering on the subject'.[14]

The iconography and poetry of the South Sea Bubble attests to the involvement of women as investors in one of the earliest stock market crashes. Jonathan Swift's satiric poem, 'The Bubble' (1720) mocks the 'Female Troops' who 'Come here their Losses to retrieve;/Ride over the Waves in spacious Hoops,/Like *Lapland* Witches in a sieve', while Edward Ward's 'South-Sea Ballad, or Merry Remarks upon Exchange-Alley Bubbles' describes

> Our greatest Ladies hither come,
> And ply in Chariots daily,
> Oft pawn their Jewels for a Sum,
> To venture in the Alley.[15]

The Alley here refers to Exchange or Change Alley in London: the vibrant site of stock trading among coffee houses of the seventeenth and eighteenth centuries. Like the playing cards this book opened with, these satirical depictions of women falling prey to the calamities of a bubble nonetheless also point to the fact that 'women consistently accounted for approximately 20 percent of the investors in major stock and bank funds'.[16] Studies of early modern ledger and household accounts further demonstrate the financial involvement and power of women, especially in domestic management (it is worth remembering the roots of economics in the Greek *oikonomia*: household governance).[17]

Adopting a 'hermeneutics of suspicion', feminist economists have challenged the false universality of *homo economicus* revealing that women are not only frequently marginalised within economic systems, but also within the discipline's core principles and concepts. The grand narrative of *homo economicus* envisions the primary role and action of the economic agent as going into the market 'exist[ing] solely in the sphere of exchange', but this obviously fails to take account of the plethora of economic activities undertaken by individuals, families, and communities, including the important work of social reproduction that is necessary to maintain the 'invisible hand' of the market. *Homo economicus* has social costs, and the narrative of maximising self-interest within the supposedly scientific domain of choice ignores the differential analytical categories of gender, race, ethnicity, and nationhood.[18] Behavioural and identity economics have recently attempted to further challenge economic orthodoxy by incorporating the social and psychological influences and consequences shaping economic behaviour. Drawing on the work of Herbert Simon ('bounded rationality'), Vernon L. Smith ('ecological rationality'), and Harvey Leibenstein ('selective rationality'), behavioural economists have complicated the definition of rationality by studying more closely what actually motivates economic decisions and the limits of rationality, how people frequently misjudge economic consequences, and how we are not always effective in the ways we adapt our economic behaviour to changing circumstances.[19] Even the conservative economic historian Niall Ferguson has acknowledged that the 'true *homo economicus*' remains a rare and 'rather monstrous' concept: 'Every day, men and women subordinate their economic self-interest to some other motive, be it the urge to play, to idle, to copulate, to wreck'.[20] Identity economics has questioned the individualised narrative attached to *homo economicus* by focusing on the social contexts and motivations that inform economic actions and decisions. Despite these attempts to widen and reframe *homo economicus*' character, identity economics remains wedded to the mathematical, the calculative, and the classificatory with its determination to fit human identities and norms within the 'utility function' (motivation) framework of economics.[21]

Coinciding with the emergence of political economy and the concept of a liberal, sovereign economic subject, the British novel can pose compelling counternarratives to the mathematically bound character narratives of economics. With its studied focus and development of character, the novel constantly demonstrates the failure of human behaviour to be defined by or contained within utility functions. Consider, for example, the transformation of Pip in Charles Dickens' *Great Expectations* (1861) from unwitting convict-rescuer to a 'gentleman' maximising his self-interest to attempted convict-rescuer and economic exile. Or the role inversion between John Thornton and Margaret Hale in Elizabeth Gaskell's *North and South* (1855) from industrial capitalist zealot and stout political economy critic, respectively, to economic austerity pennant and capital investor. Even the character most lauded (and consequently, abused) by neoclassical economics, Robinson Crusoe, betrays the limits of *homo economicus*. While neoclassical economics has frequently used Crusoe as an analogy of the economic archetype making decisions at the margin to maximise his self-interest, this narrow reading of the novel and its celebrated individualism fails to take account of the imperialist and colonialist mindset that underpins Crusoe's possessive and entitled behaviour. As postcolonial, feminist, and decolonial scholars have shown, Crusoe does not expand the wealth of his island empire in isolation but through the enslavement of Friday whose servitude he exploits for his own economic gain. Nor can we separate Crusoe's narrative gains from the historical context of the expanding British Empire and the trade in enslaved persons in which his shipwrecked-journey begins, despite economics textbooks' efforts to decontextualise Crusoe through their reliance on the escape clause of the 'hypothetical model'.[22] As Sylvia Wynter has warned, it is too easy to move from the hypothetical to the universal, such that the seemingly innocent, hypothetical economic man 'overrepresents itself as if it were the human itself'.[23] Turning to fiction gives play to the fictions within grand narratives that their claims to universality ignore. *Homo economicus* creates a generic paperchain of the individual that is then used to populate economic models and policies that have real world implications for people who would never fit the shape of the paper cut-out. Challenging the grand narrative of carbon-copy, self-interest maximisers, and countering the 'homogenizing epistemology of economics' is crucial if economics is ever going to be able to reckon with the socio-economic injustices within the world.[24]

Stadial Theory and the Industrial Revolution

The imperial, colonial, and racial implications of *homo economicus* become even clearer when we situate the model within another universalising grand narrative of economics: the stadial theory of civilisational progress. Like his Enlightenment philosopher contemporaries, David Hume and Adam Ferguson, Smith developed a theory of economic progress across four 'ages' which he identified as beginning with 'the age of hunters', progressing to 'the age of shepherds', followed by 'the age of agriculture', and concluding with 'the age of commerce naturally succeed[ing] that of agriculture'.[25] *Homo economicus* entering the marketplace and making rational economic choices according to their self-interest aligns most readily with the age of commerce, and therefore we can see how these grand narratives combine to reassert their logics of naturalised economic behaviour. While stadial theory provides a means of analysing the past through *conjectural* history, it reads history through a Eurocentric framework that centres international trade and commerce as the pinnacle of human progress and thereby treats other forms of economic activity and socio-cultural behaviour as inferior or 'primitive'. Through its preference for agriculture and commerce, stadial theory also promotes settlement over nomadism in ways that could be and (fundamentally were) co-opted by efforts to secure imperial and colonial expansion. As postcolonial economic scholars Eiman O. Zein-Elabdin and S. Charusheela have argued: 'as a "science" of material accumulation' economics is 'epistemologically comfortable with the notion of colonialism and imperial domination' and has 'historically authorized and celebrated the exploitation and colonization of natural and human communities' across the globe.[26] It is worth remembering that while he encouraged free trade and commerce, Smith cautioned against the excesses of the age of commerce and the 'master manufacturers' who believed it reasonable that they have the 'monopoly of the ingenuity of all their countrymen'.[27] Nonetheless it is also possible to see how the narrative of mastery over nature that accompanies the narrative of stadial theory feeds into an expansionary vision of commerce through the productive capacities of the division of labour and the later industrial 'revolution'. This grand narrative of mastery and civilisation is also tied to a narrative of modernity that 'conflate[s] Europe with modernity and render[s] the process of becoming modern, at least in the first instance, one of endogenous European development' while at the same time excluding the rest of the world from these 'world-historical processes' and dismissing 'colonial connections' as 'insignificant to their development'.[28] The four-step process of the stadial theory has also been 'progressively' remapped onto the history of capitalism in recent historiographies as commercial capitalism, competitive capitalism, state-managed capitalism, and concluding with financialised capitalism and the contemporary manifestations of romanticised hype and revolutionary mythmaking in the new economy of digital finance capitalism.[29]

Classical economics' stadial narrative of modernising progress has, however, been marked by fears of stagnation that recognised the impossibility of continuous growth. Concerned about the effects of the growing population rates on increases in poverty, eighteenth-century political economist Thomas Malthus famously warned against the impending exhaustion of resources supporting human life because population growth and food production operated on different growth ratios: population as a geometrical ratio increases by multiplication, whereas, food increases by addition and is therefore an arithmetic ratio. Malthus uses an analogy of a 'great reservoir of water' to draw out the consequences of the resource diminishment accompanying uninterrupted population growth:

> Where there are few people, and a great quantity of fertile land, the power of the earth to afford a yearly increase in food may be compared to a great reservoir of water, supplied by a moderate stream. The faster population increases, the more help will be got to draw water, and consequently an increasing quantity will be taken every year. But the sooner, undoubtedly, will the reservoir be exhausted, and the streams only remain. When acre has been added to acre, till all the fertile land is occupied, the yearly increase of food will depend on the amelioration of the land already in possession; and even this moderate stream will be gradually diminishing. But population, could it be supplied with food, would go with unexhausted vigour, and the increase of one period would furnish the power of a greater increase the next, and this without any limit.[30]

The evocative imagery of a stream running dry and the consequent drought captures the seriousness with which Malthus viewed the impending resource exhaustion and starvation if population growth went unchecked.

Though Ricardo disagreed with Malthus' proposed solutions to this issue (most crucially on the Corn Laws), his theory of rent also illustrated a law of diminishing returns. Rent is only ever paid for the use of land because 'land is of different qualities with respect to its productive powers, and because in the progress of population, land of inferior quality, or less advantageously situated, is called into cultivation'. As society progresses through population growth and 'land of the second degree of fertility is taken into cultivation', rent 'immediately commences on that of the first quality' with the amount of rent dependent on the 'difference in the quality of these two portions of land'.[31] Ricardo's concerns about diminishing returns were at their most amplified in response to the possibility of a stationary state—where growth stalls; neither increasing or declining—a possibility which he described as a 'retrograde condition' and an 'unnatural state of society':

> Man from youth grows to manhood, then decays, and dies; but this is not the progress of nations. When arrived to a state of the greatest vigour, their further advance may indeed be arrested, but their natural tendency is to continue for the ages, to sustain undiminished their wealth, and their population.[32]

Ricardo's fear of the retrograde condition of the stationary state is evident in his circumscribing it to a 'far distant' possibility.[33] The stationary state is a haunting, but not an immediately asserted, presence throughout Ricardo's *Principles*. Not so for his successor, J. S. Mill, however, who argued that no 'progressive movement' is 'in its nature unlimited', asking his readers: 'Towards what ultimate point is society tending by its industrial progress? When the progress ceases, in what condition are we to expect that it will leave mankind?' Mill proceeds to chastise his fellow political economists, arguing that

> It must always have been seen, more or less distinctly, by political economists, that the increase of wealth is not boundless: that at the end of what they term the progressive state lies the stationary state, that all progress in wealth is but a postponement of this, and that each step in advance is an approach to it.

Critiquing his colleagues for focusing solely on 'all that is economically desirable with the progressive state, and with that alone', Mill returns us to Malthus' metaphor of the stream, describing the stationary state as 'this irresistible necessity that the stream of human industry should finally spread itself out into an apparently stagnant sea'. Avoiding the stationary state is impossible according to Mill, and therefore, a more important question is how to get to the 'best state for human nature' where 'while no one is poor, no one desires to be richer, nor has any reason to fear being thrust back, by the efforts of others to push themselves forward'.[34] As Gareth Dale argues, Mill's stationary state is a 'remarkable departure in classical political economy and a distinguished addition to the literature of utopia'.[35] Even within the nineteenth-century Industrial Revolution discourse of celebrated expansion, narratives of stagnation and exhaustion accompanied those of growth and development. A repository of triumphalist narratives of British ingenuity, distinctiveness, and progress, the Industrial Revolution is, nonetheless, a site of theoretical contestation regarding the legacies of class exploitation and British inventiveness. The historian Arnold Toynbee was the first to popularise the phrase the Industrial Revolution in English in his posthumously published, *Lectures on the Industrial Revolution* (1884), in which he traced the history of this revolution alongside the development of political economy. Though Toynbee highlighted the growth in population, the 'substitution of the factory for the domestic system', and transition to new energy forms such as coal and steam, accompanied by the all-important technological change through the inventions of the spinning-jenny, power-loom, and steam engine, he was also deeply concerned by the growth of pauperism, claiming that the 'problem of pauperism came upon men in its most terrible form between 1795 and 1834' and that the 'effects of the Industrial Revolution prove that free competition may produce wealth without producing well-being'.[36] While not denying the escape from the Malthusian stagnation trap the Industrial Revolution could provide, it is important to complicate the story of growth and the launching of the working class into middle-class prosperity frequently associated with the 'revolution'. Although studies of real wages indicate a gradual increase across the nineteenth century, other indicators such as life expectancy and child mortality tell a story of 'concurrent worsening living conditions', such that the moment at which Britain

> finally broke free from the constraints of the organic economy, was not a time of rising prosperity for all, but a period of painful transition which brought few gains for the men, women and children whose back-breaking labour underpinned it.[37]

The dialectic of progress and decline, enrichment and impoverishment was so stark, for example, that in his preface to the 1892 edition of *The Condition of the Working-Class in England*, Friedrich Engels would ask:

> If even under the unparalleled commercial and industrial expansion, from 1848 to 1866, they have had to undergo such misery; if even then the great bulk of them experienced at best but a temporary improvement of their condition, while only a small, privileged, 'protected' minority was permanently benefited, what will it be when this dazzling period is brought finally to a close; when the present dreary stagnation shall not only become intensified, but this, its intensified condition, shall become the permanent and normal state of English trade?[38]

As Elizabeth C. Miller has shown, a 'mood of finitude' is pervasive across the British Empire's extraction ecologies and 'industrial Britain was never without an ever-present sense that it was living on borrowed time'.[39] The distinctive inventiveness of British industrialism has equally faced recent challenges, with work by Jenny Bulstrode undermining the legitimacy of ironmaster and 'revolution maker' Henry Cort's patenting of the 'Cort process' which allowed for the mass production of wrought-iron. Bulstrode's research instead demonstrates that the process for which 'Cort took credit' was actually developed by '76 Black metallurgists from Jamaica'.[40] Through her research, Bulstrode pushes us to question the stadial association of Europe with modernity and industrialisation and to 'change whose history gets promoted—to move beyond the clamour of patents and priority claims that serve hegemonic groups; and perhaps, in doing so, to identify truly innovative ideas and applications based on use'.[41]

While the dates and the environmental and socio-economic consequences of the transition from agrarian to industrial capitalism continue to be a site of much scholarly debate and tension, there is no doubt that the narrative of progress accompanying stadial theory is being re/contested in the face of climate change, extinction discourse, and impending ecological collapse. Jason Moore challenges us to reconsider 'humanity's modern relation with the rest of nature' and the 'origins of ecological crises' as not beginning with the Anthropocene's time frames—which range in beginnings, from the arrival of the steam engine and the Industrial Revolution to the 1945 'Great Acceleration'—but with what he refers to as the Capitalocene. This is 'a system of power, profit, and re/production in the web of life' and an 'environment-making revolution' that Moore dates to 1450; a period that saw the imperial expansion of agrarian capitalism and primitive accumulation that accompanied the conquest and colonisation of the Americas in the early modern period.[42] This reframing of the origin stories of environmental crises ask us to think of anthropogenic climate change not as a 'novelty' but rather as part of the 'historical *continuity* of dispossession and disaster caused by empire'.[43]

The imperial epistemologies that underpin the stadial thinking of modernity and progress have long been challenged by Indigenous peoples, and postcolonial and decolonial movements who view anthropogenic climate change as an 'intensification of [the] environmental change imposed on indigenous peoples by colonialism'.[44] Initially formulated by Cedric J. Robinson, the concept of 'racial capitalism' emphasises the non-objectivity of capitalist development and has received renewed attention by scholars critiquing the homogenising and universalising tendencies of the Anthropocene as a concept that fails to take account of the uneven distribution of its consequences and the legacies of imperialism, colonialism, and racial capitalism that structure this unevenness. Arguing for the recognition of the *racial* capitalocene, Françoise Vergès reads Robinson in conjunction with Moore to identify the global colour line as a structuring component of climate change.[45] Environmental activists and historians, such as Vandana Shiva and Rob Nixon, have also long pointed to the existence and persistence of environmental racism, and many scholars are now emphasising the centrality of racialised environments to any analysis of altered ecologies and ecosystems. Potawatomi scholar-activists Kyle Whyte and Robin Wall Kimmerer have demonstrated, for example, how important traditional ecological knowledge (TEK) is to the holistic management of environments and adaptation to climate change. 'Decolonising the Anthropocene', Whyte argues that 'Indigenous climate change studies perform futurities that Indigenous persons can build on in generations to come'.[46] Following the devastating 2020 Australian bushfires in which an estimated 17 million hectares of bushland was burnt, 33 deaths were directly caused by the fires, and over 3,000 homes were lost, there have been calls to restore and learn from Indigenous fire management systems that have been practised for generations. Investigations into the 'ways in which the traditional land and fire management practices of Indigenous Australians could improve Australia's resilience to natural disasters' were written into the remit of the bushfires Royal Commission.[47] Furthermore, research has shown how the loss of Indigenous fire management and cultural burning practices in northern Australia has led to the collapse of Gondwana conifer populations.[48] What this work shows is that the Eurocentric focus on grand narratives of the teleological march towards scientific and industrial modernity frequently misses significant counternarratives and alternative systems of knowledge.

Homo economicus is also revealed to be the wrong actor for this period of polycrises as they are incapable of managing or responding to the scale of the risks associated with climate change. The attachment to cost-benefit analysis deprives *homo economicus* of the ability to assess our period's 'radical risks'. As Dipesh Chakrabarty has shown the risk and short-term probability assessments that have lent the economics discipline so well to the 'art of social management', mean that it is ill-fitted to understanding the unpredictability of climate system tipping points or undertaking the scalar thinking necessary to respond effectively:

> [T]heir methods are such that they appear to hold or bracket climate change as a broadly known variable (converting its uncertainties into risks that have been acknowledged and evaluated) while working out options that humans can create for themselves striving together or even wrangling among themselves. The world climate system, in other words, has no significant capacity to be a wild card in their calculations in so far as they can make policy prescriptions; it is there in a relatively predictable form to be managed by human ingenuity and political mobilisation.[49]

It is clear from the references to human ingenuity and management that the narrative of mastery carries over to the discipline's responses to climate catastrophe: unwieldy nature must be re-tamed, trained, and controlled by the grand narrative of human progress. Or to flip this narrative and follow Iyko Day (channelling Fredric Jameson): it appears 'easier to imagine the end of the world than the end of capitalism'.[50]

The Great Divergence, Convergence, and Degrowth

Coined by Samuel Huntington, the 'Great Divergence' is a compound grand narrative: it both builds on and reinforces the developmental narratives of modernising *homo economicus* and his stadial accomplishments. Effectively captured by the slogans 'the rise of the West' and 'the West and the rest', the Great Divergence aims to theorise the apparent explosive economic growth and development of eighteenth and nineteenth-century Western Europe which saw it come to dominate the 'rest of the world', but especially drawing a stark contrast with the nineteenth-century economic stagnation of China and Japan. Significant scholarly disagreements about the dating of this economic split continue depending on the causes of divergence cited: for example, those claiming 'cultural' or 'institutional' differences as the primary causes of developmental separation frequently trace the starting point to the fifteenth and sixteenth centuries. Kenneth Pomeranz, by contrast, aims to counter the Eurocentric narrative of cultural and institutional 'exceptionalism'. Relying on standard of living markers such as life expectancy, calorie consumption, as well as data of productivity and earnings, Pomeranz argues that the areas most advanced in China matched or even surpassed those in Europe until the early nineteenth century, such that what are thought to be 'unique European achievements look more and more ordinary'.[51] The 'Great Divergence' of the nineteenth century for Pomeranz is, instead, traceable to the resource extractive possibilities provided by the New World, the trade in enslaved peoples, and the move to fossil fuels, which allowed Europe to escape 'the land constraint'.[52]

Pomeranz is not, of course, the first to point to the significant role the colonies played in capitalist accumulation and development in Europe. Although tracing a longer history, Marx found plunder to be part of the 'historical material' of the merchant's capital:

> Commercial capital, when it holds a dominant position, is thus in all cases a system of plunder, just as its development in the trading peoples of both ancient and modern times is directly bound up with violent plunder, piracy, the taking of slaves and the subjugation of colonies.

Marx is damning:

> With the development of capitalist production during the period of manufacture, the public opinion of Europe lost its last remnant of shame and

conscience. The nations bragged cynically of every infamy that served them as a means to the accumulation of capital.

Conquest, slavery, and robbery were a foundational part of the 'secret of primitive accumulation' for Marx: following the Asiento Treaty, 'Liverpool grew fat on the basis of the slave trade'.[53] Scholarship from the first half of the twentieth century has equally been crucial in challenging the Eurocentric arc of development. French economic historian Henri Sée demonstrated in the 1920s, for example, the 'pivotal role' the French West Indian colonies played in the capital accumulation of France, while the work of W. E. B. Du Bois and C. L. R. James has been crucial in revising the narrative of Western Europe's capitalist growth to be dependent on the enslavement of African people.[54] The recent calls by scholars, activists, and even a leading judge in the international court of justice, Judge Patrick Robinson, to make reparations a key talking point of Britain's future international relations policy is testament to the long economic legacies of the slave trade and the problematic framing of the Great Divergence.

The narrative of the Great Divergence generates its own future counternarrative of the Great Convergence where, the argument goes, developing economies of the 'Global South' will eventually 'catch-up' with the advanced economies of the 'Global North'. Following a modernisation story, the Great Convergence theory argues that incomes of developing and advanced economies converge through the spread of industrialisation and modernisation, with developing economies' growth increasing sharply while the growth of advanced economies' either stagnates or declines. The hierarchy of inventiveness, exceptionalism, and responsibility for the Great Convergence is clear: 'early developers create technologies which others can learn, purchase or steal. Since the adaptation of new methods of production is likely to be cheaper than their discovery, latecomers have an inbuilt advantage and can fast-track their development'.[55] This pattern of learnt-behavioural growth lends itself well, as Alfredo Saad-Filho has demonstrated, to the implementation of the Structural Adjustment programmes informed by the neoliberal principles of the 'Washington Consensus' of the 1980s—fiscal discipline and austerity, privatisation, and trade liberalisation: 'In order to converge, [developing economies] must adopt the "correct" economic policies and implement the "necessary" structural reforms'.[56] The failure of structural adjustment to lead to the expected growth outcomes projected by its institutional hegemons, the International Monetary Fund and the World Bank, has been problematically blamed on the failure of developing economies to implement the neoliberal adjustment policies correctly—a 'logical inversion' that 'renders conventional policies and neoclassical growth theory immune to criticism'.[57]

While the notion of global economies converging in terms of wealth distribution would be a welcome development in so much as it suggested a more equal and just world, the evidence in support of the Great Convergence has been widely contested. Actual convergence seems limited to a handful of countries such as China and India. But even the optimism associated with the economic promise and stability of the BRICS (Brazil, Russia, India, China, and South Africa) seems misplaced. Rather, as Sahan Savas Karatasli and Sefika Kumral argue,

> What we have been observing since the 1990s—namely the rise of China, India, and a cluster of peripheral countries from the Global South—is not a Great Convergence but another Great Divergence process linked to US-led financialization and the current crisis of capitalism.[58]

Similarly, Saad-Filho has pointed to the combined yet uneven development where 'unprecedented prosperity' has been created for some countries and regions, 'while others have declined in relative and even in absolute terms'.[59] Moreover, as the Marxist geographer, David Harvey, has frequently noted, capitalist accumulation continues to function through a process of dispossession which works through the 'spatial fix' in which capital moves from exhausted centres of capital accumulation and stagnation to new geographical regions where the cycle of accumulation can begin anew or in a newly aggressive fashion: 'The general thrust of any capitalistic logic of power is not that territories should be held back from capitalist development, but that they should be continuously opened up'.[60] The technological advance that is seen as so integral to the modernising trajectory of the Great Convergence is also key to this 'accumulation by dispossession' where 'capitalism can utilize its powers of technological change and investment to induce unemployment (lay-offs) thus creating an industrial reserve army of unemployed workers directly'.[61]

The convergence aspiration has been more thoroughly rejected recently by supporters of degrowth who question the logic of economic growth as a desirable ambition. Emphasising the need for a more just and equal distribution of wealth that also takes account of the environmental and ecological consequences of a development narrative that focuses primarily on Gross Domestic Product, proponents of degrowth instead focus on (among other things) the possibilities of redistribution rather than more consumption; regenerative agricultural practices rather than mass production; investment in renewable energy sources accompanied by the divestment in fossil fuel economies; and debt cancellation rather than more economic policies framed around adjustment toward neoclassical growth patterns. Degrowth is a fundamental rejection of the foundational premises of neoclassical and neoliberal economics that returns us to the counternarratives of exhaustion and stagnation that questioned the nineteenth-century expansionary visions of the Industrial Revolution. A multivalent, normative concept, degrowth challenges the developmental paradigm that structures the Great Divergence and Convergence by recognising the legacies of exploitation that have underpinned and continue to support growth rates. While there are numerous schools of thought within the degrowth movement, they all aim for the democratisation of the global economy but are crucially not about making 'GDP growth negative', i.e. resulting in a recession. Rather, in focusing on the improvement and sustainability of 'social and environmental conditions', the GDP predictably declines under degrowth policies because of the economic redistribution that prioritises social welfare, universal basic income, and progressive tax reform.[62] Gaining global momentum, the degrowth movement nonetheless remains outside the conventional economic centres driving national economic policies, limiting its ability to change national, let alone, international economic frameworks. Yet degrowth's de-centred position is also what allows it to imagine radical futures that dismantle economic growth fixtures.

***

The foundational stories of economics are shakier than ever. Calls for a more just and ecologically sustainable world are challenging the grand narratives of political economy even while the concentration of wealth among individual billionaires continues to have startling consequences for how we imagine the political and economic sovereignty of nation states. It is crucial that we continue to revisit the histories of our current economic thinking as—given they are equally marked by fears of exhaustion, stagnation, and inequality and are plagued by environmental devastation and plunder—they can inform a reimagining of our economic aspirations as more ecologically and socially just.

Notes

1 Adam Smith, *The Wealth of Nations: Complete and Unabridged*, ed. Edwin Cannan and intro. Robert Reich (New York: Random House, 2000), IV.II, 482, 484.
2 Smith, *Wealth of Nations*, IV.II, 485.
3 Smith, *Wealth of Nations*, V.I, 766. For a more detailed discussion of the history of economics and 'the passions', see Albert O. Hirschman, *The Passions and the Interests* (Princeton: Princeton University Press, 1977).
4 Claudia C. Klaver, *A/Moral Economics: Classical Political Economy and Cultural Authority in Nineteenth Century England* (Columbus: Ohio State University Press, 2003), 9; Smith, *Wealth of Nations*, II.II, 320–321.
5 Smith, *Wealth of Nations*, II.III, 371.
6 John Stuart Mill, *Principles of Political Economy with Some of Their Applications to Social Philosophy*, ed. and intro. William James Ashley, 7th ed. (London: Longmans, Green and Co., 1923), 1, III.I, 438, III.XVIII, 588, III.XXIV, 655.
7 Mill, *Principles*, IV.IV, 730.
8 John Maynard Keynes, *The General Theory of Employment, Interest, and Money*, intro. Paul Krugman (London: Macmillan for the Royal Economic Society, 2007), 162–163.

9 Ayn Rand, *Atlas Shrugged* (London: Penguin Books, 2007), 798.
10 Gore Vidal, 'Comment, July 1961', *Esquire* 1961, http://www.esquire.com/features/gore-vidal-archive/comment-0761; Whittaker Chambers, 'Big Sister Is Watching You', *National Review*, 28 November 1957, 596.
11 For more on Rand's political and economic influence see Jennifer Burns, *Goddess of the Market: Ayn Rand and the American Right* (Oxford: Oxford University Press, 2009); Sarah Comyn, *Political Economy and the Novel* (London: Palgrave Macmillan, 2018).
12 Gary S. Becker, *Human Capital: A Theoretical and Empirical Analysis, with Special Reference to Education*, 3rd ed. (Chicago: The University of Chicago Press, 1993), 11, (emphasis mine).
13 Susan F. Feiner, 'A Portrait of Homo Economicus as a Young Man', in *The New Economic Criticism: Studies at the Intersection of Literature and Economics*, ed. Martha Woodmansee and Mark Osteen (London: Routledge, 1999), 194; Marianne A. Ferber and Julie A. Nelson, eds., *Beyond Economic Man: Feminist Theory and Economics* (Chicago: University of Chicago Press, 1993), 4.
14 Maria Edgeworth, 'To Mrs. Ruxton, 9 March 1822', in *Letters from England, 1813–1844*, ed. Christina Colvin (London: Oxford University Press, 1971), 364.
15 Jonathan Swift, *The Bubble: A Poem* (London: Ben Tooke, 1721), l. 97–100; Edward Ward, *A South-Sea Ballad, or, Merry Remarks Upon Exchange-Alley Bubbles* (Dublin: s.l., 1720).
16 Catherine Ingrassia, *Authorship, Commerce, and Gender in Early Eighteenth-Century England: A Culture of Paper Credit* (Cambridge: Cambridge University Press, 1998), 2.
17 See, for example, Alexandra Shepard, 'Crediting Women in Early Modern English Economy', *History Workshop Journal* 79, no. 1 (2015), 1–24; Adam Smyth, 'Money, Accounting, and Life-Writing, 1600–1700: Balancing a Life', *A History of English Autobiography*, ed. Adam Smyth (Cambridge: Cambridge University Press, 2016), 86–99.
18 Drucilla K. Barker and Susan F. Feiner, ' "Economics", She Wrote', in *Liberating Economics: Feminist Perspectives on Families, Work, and Globalization* (Ann Arbor: University of Michigan Press, 2004), 1–18 (8, 5).
19 For an excellent introduction to behavioural economics, see Michelle Baddeley, *Behavioural Economics: A Very Short Introduction* (Oxford: Oxford University Press, 2017).
20 Niall Ferguson, *The Cash Nexus: Money and Power in the Modern World, 1700–2000* (London: Allen Lane, 2001), 424–425.
21 George A. Akerlof and Rachel E. Kranton, *Identity Economics: How Our Identities Shape Our Work, Wages, and Well-Being* (Princeton: Princeton University Press, 2010).
22 Matthew Watson, 'Rousseau's Crusoe Myth: The Unlikely Provenance of the Neoclassical *homo economicus*', *Journal of Cultural Economy* 10, no. 1 (2017), 81–96.
23 Sylvia Wynter, 'Unsettling the Coloniality of Being/Power/Truth/Freedom: Towards the Human, After Man, Its Overrepresentation—An

Argument', *CR: The New Centennial Review* 3, no. 3 (2003), 257–337 (260), cited in Watson, 'Rousseau's Crusoe Myth'.
24 Eiman O. Zein-Elabdin and S. Charusheela, 'Introduction: Economics and Postcolonial Thought', in *Postcolonialism Meets Economics*, ed. S. Charusheela and Eiman O. Zein-Elabdin (London and New York: Routledge, 2004), 1–18 (8).
25 Adam Smith, *Lectures on Jurisprudence*, ed. R. L. Meel, D. D. Raphael, and P. G. Stein (Oxford: Oxford University Press, 1978), 14, 459.
26 Zein-Elabdin and Charusheela, 'Introduction', 2.
27 Smith, *Wealth of Nations*, IV.VIII, 715.
28 Gurminder K. Bhambra, 'Modernity: History of a Concept', in *International Encyclopedia of the Social and Behavioural Sciences*, ed. James D. Wright, 2nd ed. (Oxford: Elsevier, 2015), 692–696 (692).
29 Gurminder K. Bhambra, 'Colonial Global Economy: Towards a Theoretical Reorientation of Political Economy', *Review of International Political Economy* 28, no. 2 (2021), 307–322 (309). See also Nancy Fraser and Rahel Jaeggi, *Capitalism: A Conversation in Critical Theory* (Cambridge and Oxford: Polity Press, 2018).
30 Thomas Malthus, *An Essay on the Principle of Population, as It Affects the Future Improvement of Society, with Remarks on the Speculations of Mr. Godwin, M. Condorcet, and Other Writers* (London: J. Johnson, 1798), 107–108.
31 David Ricardo, *The Works and Correspondence of David Ricardo: I: On the Principles of Political Economy and Taxation*, ed. Piero Sraffa and M. H. Dobb (Cambridge: Cambridge University Press, 1951), 70.
32 Ricardo, *The Works and Correspondence of David Ricardo*, 265.
33 Ricardo, *The Works and Correspondence of David Ricardo*, 109.
34 Mill, *Principles*, IV.IV, 746.
35 Gareth Dale, 'Critiques of Growth in Classical Political Economy: Mill's Stationary State and a Marxian Response', *New Political Economy* 18, no. 3 (2013), 431–457 (440).
36 Arnold Toynbee, *Lectures on the Industrial Revolution of the Eighteenth Century in England: Popular Addresses, Notes, and other Fragments*, new ed. with reminiscence of Lord Milner (London: Longmans, Green and Co., 1908), 69, 73–74.
37 Emma Griffin, *A Short History of the British Industrial Revolution* (Basingstoke: Palgrave Macmillan, 2010), 160–161.
38 Friedrich Engels, *The Condition of the Working-Class in England in 1844, with Preface Written in 1892*, trans. Florence Kelley Wischnewetzky (London: Swan Sonnenschein and Co., 1892), xvii.
39 Elizabeth C. Miller, *Extraction Ecologies and the Long History of Exhaustion* (Princeton: Princeton University Press, 2021), 8, 11.
40 Jenny Bulstrode, 'Black Metallurgists and the Making of the Industrial Revolution', *History and Technology* 39, no. 1 (2023), 1–41 (2).
41 Bulstrode, 'Black Metallurgists', 2.
42 Jason Moore, 'The Capitalocene, Part I: On the Nature and Origins of Our Ecological Crisis', *The Journal of Peasant Studies* 44, no. 3 (2017), 594–630 (606).

43 Elizabeth DeLoughrey, *Allegories of the Anthropocene* (Durham and London: Duke University Press, 2019), 2.
44 Kyle Whyte, 'Indigenous Climate Change Studies: Indigenizing Futures, Decolonizing the Anthropocene', *English Language Notes* 55, no. 1–2 (2017), 153–162 (153).
45 Françoise Vergès, 'Racial Capitalocene', in *Futures of Black Radicalism*, ed. Gaye Theresa Johnson and Alex Lubin (London: Verso, 2017), 72–81.
46 Whyte, 'Indigenous Climate Change', 160.
47 B. Williamson, 'Cultural Burning and Public Forests: Convergences and Divergences Between Aboriginal Groups and Forest Management in South-Eastern Australia', *Australian Forestry* 85, no. 1 (2022), 1–5 (1).
48 David Bowman et al., 'Population Collapse of a Gondwanan Conifer Follows the Loss of Indigenous Fire Regimes in a Northern Australian Savanna', *Scientific Reports* 12, no. 9081 (2022), https://hdl.handle.net/102.100.100/550570
49 Dipesh Chakrabarty, 'Climate and Capital: On Conjoined Histories', *Critical Inquiry* 41, no. 1 (2014), 1–23 (4–5).
50 Iyko Day, 'Ruin Porn and the Colonial Imaginary', *PMLA* 36, no. 1 (2021), 125–131 (125).
51 Kenneth Pomeranz, *The Great Divergence: China, Europe, and the Making of the Modern World Economy* (Princeton: Princeton University Press, 2000), 11.
52 Pomeranz, *The Great Divergence*, 265–297.
53 Karl Marx, *Capital Volume 3*, intro. Ernest Mandel and trans. David Fernbach (London and New York: Penguin Classics, 1991), 448–449.
54 For an excellent account of this scholarly history see Kaveh Yazdani and Constanza Castro, 'Capitalisms of the "Global South" (c. 10th to 19th Centuries)—Old and New Contributions and Debates', *Historia and Crítica* 89 (2023), 3–41.
55 Alfredo Saad-Filho, 'The "Rise of the South": Global Convergence at Last?', *New Political Economy* 19, no. 4 (2014), 578–600 (580).
56 Saad-Filho, 'The Rise of the South', 581.
57 Saad-Filho, 'The Rise of the South', 583.
58 Sahan Savas Karataşli and Sefika Kumral, 'Great Convergence or the Third Great Divergence? Changes in the Global Distribution of Wealth, 1500–2008', in *The World-System as a Unit of Analysis*, ed. Robert Patricio Korzeniewicz (New York: Routledge, 2017), 36–49 (38).
59 Saad-Filho, 'The Rise of the South', 595.
60 David Harvey, *The New Imperialism* (Oxford: Oxford University Press, 2003), 139.
61 Harvey, *The New Imperialism*, 141.
62 For an introduction to the principles of the degrowth movement see, for example, Giorgis Kallis, *Degrowth* (Newcastle upon Tyne: Agenda Publishing, 2018); Matthias Schmelzer, Andrea Vetter, and Aaron Vansintjan, *The Future Is Degrowth: A Guide to a World Beyond Capitalism* (London: Verso, 2022).

3 Currency

On 27 February 1797, in an effort to curb the panic following an attempted (but defeated) invasion of Wales by the French, the Bank of England issued an extraordinary public notice announcing a suspension to the conversion of its notes from paper into specie. While aiming to reassure the

> proprietors of BANK STOCK, as well as the PUBLICK at large, that the general Concerns of the BANK are in the most affluent and prosperous Situation, and such as to preclude every Doubt as to the Security of its Notes,

the notice nonetheless included the order of the Privy Council that

> [i]t is the unanimous Opinion, of the Board, that it is indispensably necessary for the Publick Service, that the Directors of the Bank of England, should forbear issuing any Cash in Payment until the Sense of Parliament can be taken on the subject.[1]

This initial notice was followed by the official passing of the Bank Restriction Act on 8 May 1797 which enforced the suspension, and therefore, deferral of note convertibility. At first intended to only be in place for several weeks, the Act and what came to be known as the Bank Restriction Period in fact lasted until 1821, a period of almost 25 years.

The purpose of the Act was to forestall a run on the Bank of England, address and halt panic, secure the Bank's assets, and instil a sense of trust in the Bank's financial bulwarks. The suspension of convertibility created, however, a different sort of panic: an anxiety about the meaning of money and the relationship between a currency's representational value and its *actual* value secured through its association with either gold or silver. Divorced from the stability provided by the Bank's bullion, paper currency seemed to become a free-floating signifier, worth only the value of its paper, rather than the amounts indicated by its ink inscriptions. James Gillray's hand-coloured etching, *Midas, Transmuting all into Paper* (1797, Figure 3.1) satirises the disconnect between Prime Minister Pitt (wearing asses' ears and sitting astride

DOI: 10.4324/9781003281627-4

52 *Currency*

the Bank) asserting his 'power to secure public credit' and the public's dismay at seeing the Midas reversal of the nation's gold become excrement—paper currency as bodily waste, paper spittle polluting the skies while the Bank's vaults are hollowed out and transformed into a latrine.

The value of the Bank of England notes was further compromised during the Restriction Period due to the exponential rise in forgery caused by the 'massive expansion of paper money' of reduced quality necessitated by the

Figure 3.1 James Gillray, *Midas, Transmuting all into Paper*, London 1797. © The Trustees of the British Museum. Used with permission.

suspension of convertibility. The Restriction Act 'authorised the mass production of new £1 and £2 banknotes' to replace the specie no longer circulating and as these new banknotes were of poorer quality they could be more easily forged. Coupled with the fact that a 'class of people wholly unfamiliar with paper credit' were using these notes for the first time, they could unknowingly be given and pass on counterfeit currency—a prosecutable offence known as 'uttering'.[2] As a consequence of one of the most draconian forms of legislation during this period—capital punishment for forgery or transportation for possessing or passing on a forged note—the Restriction Period saw, according to Phil Handler, 'over 2000 prosecutions and over 300 executions' for forgery, while 'the period 1783–97 saw only four prosecutions for forgery'.[3] The controversy surrounding the Restriction Act was heightened when the suspension of convertibility continued despite peace with France being achieved in 1815, and George Cruikshank's image *Bank Restriction Note, a satirical note*, (Figure 3.2) from 1819 explicitly protests the disastrous social costs of the Restriction Period. A notice under the hanging bodies of men and women reads: 'During the Issue of Bank Notes easily imitated and until Resumption of Cash Payments, or the Abolition of the Punishment of Death'. Replacing the signature of the Bank of England Governor with that of J. Ketch or Jack Ketch, the infamous English executioner during the reign of King Charles II, Cruikshank explicitly bloodies the hands of the Bank of England directors with

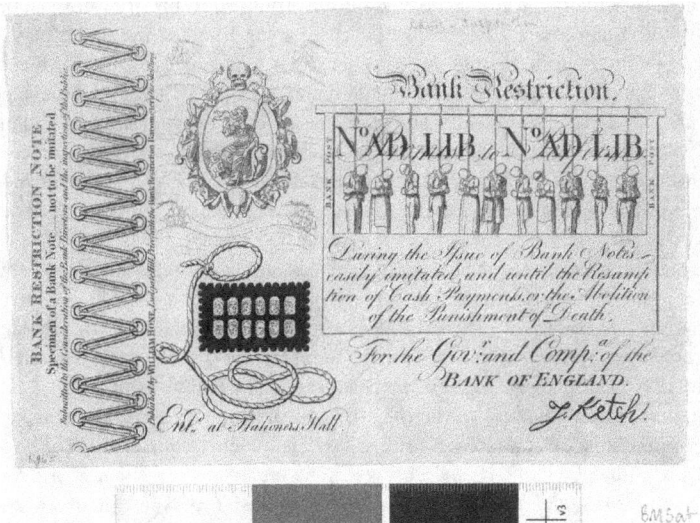

Figure 3.2 George Cruikshank, *Bank Restriction Note*, London, 1819. © The Trustees of the British Museum. Used with permission.

the deaths of those handling counterfeit notes. Indeed, Cruikshank claimed that he engraved the note of protest after seeing the bodies of executed women at the Old Bailey who had been hanged for passing on forged £1 notes.[4]

The catastrophic measures the Bank of England took to assert the credibility of *its* notes, underscores the fundamental question the Bank Restriction Act posed to British society: could the notes, as mere representations of value, still intrinsically hold that value? The nineteenth-century radical commentator William Cobbett captured the public sentiment of mistrust in the valuation of paper currency divorced from bullion when he questioned the promise inscribed on the notes: 'a promise that the Bankers . . . who issue the notes, will *pay* the notes upon *demand*'. Surely, an exasperated Cobbett demanded, this does 'not mean, the giving of *one note for another*'. The extensive subtitle of his book *Paper Against Gold* (1828) summarised his irritation and dismay with paper currency which consisted of the history of 'Other Tricks and Contrivances, carried on by the Means of Paper Money'.[5] As Kevin Barry has concluded, the bank notes became 'promises to pay promises with promises'.[6] A crisis of representation and value—what the literary historian Mary Poovey refers to as the 'problematic of representation'—thus accompanied the Bank Restriction Act, a crisis that demanded the public be able to carefully read and evaluate the circulating paper that was rapidly increasing in number.[7]

Cruikshank's satirical note showed not only the tragedy inherent to financial illiteracy, but also underscored the materiality of paper money 'as one of the most ubiquitous and one of the most overlooked forms of print media'.[8] As the Adam Smith £20 note we began Chapter 1 with demonstrates, bank notes communicate through their images, inscriptions, and associated values, conveying information beyond simple monetary value. The Smith note captured the capacity for the division of labour to power the wheel of circulation, with the print medium of currency becoming an embodiment of the force of its exchange. To put it simply: currencies tell stories. Stories about their economic and symbolic value, their exchange, their regulation, and the cultures in which they circulate. The ability to parse the multiple meanings and values of changing currencies became increasingly crucial to participating effectively in a market society. Eighteenth-century it-narratives (texts in which objects narrate the stories of their existence, often involving elaborate travels and encounters with all aspects of society, both rich and poor) became a medium in which currencies could tell their stories. The adventures of Chrysal the guinea begin, for instance, when he is dug out of a mine by a man corrupted by 'an insatiable desire of riches' and follow his travels through America, England, Holland, Germany, and Portugal.[9] The protagonist of Thomas Bridges' *The Adventures of a Bank-Note* (1770), by contrast, begins his life in a financial institution through the deposit of some minor earnings by a poet. This narrative explains to the reader how early banknotes are 'born': 'The person that deposits cash for a bank-note may properly be called its father'.[10] Already, the origins of these currencies establish their differences: Charles Johnstone's 1760 narrative of Chrysal the guinea emphasises the materiality of the coin through the depiction of the extractive labour involved in unearthing it, while Bridges' banknote (though still linked to the poet's labour and earnings) is far more abstract and institutionalised. As Poovey notes, *The Adventures* provides a 'surprising amount of information about Bank of England paper', including details about the identifying serial numbers and dates of issue, how they were circulated and finally cashed in; information narrated in an imaginative style that could potentially 'help make the Bank of England note familiar to readers who had never encountered one'.[11] Currency it-narratives also emphasise a society increasingly dominated by circulating objects, 'symbolize the promiscuous movement of text' and are 'emblematic of a burgeoning consumer culture' where the individual becomes subordinate to 'impersonal patterns of circulation'.[12] They, therefore, map the beginnings of currency's abstraction while simultaneously working as a counterpoint to this abstraction by giving a specific currency an individual voice and character despite its endless circulation.

Literature, and novels in particular, can, therefore, provide a suitable training ground for both confronting and managing the crisis of representation created by these new forms of circulating financial media. A crisis of representation and circulation that was exacerbated by the Restriction Period. Fiction continually asks its readers to assess situations, make value judgements, manage expectations, suspend disbelief, gather information and evidence, measure deceipts, trace deferrals in plot, and ultimately rewards close attention to detail. All qualities and skills that can be usefully applied during a crisis of representation: as explicit acts of representation or, alternatively, fantasy, literature teaches the importance of being able to appropriately read and evaluate representative acts and media. It is not surprising then, that the Restriction Period, as a number of scholars have noted, coincides with a significant part of the Romantic Period in literature and that many Romantic novelists and poets were reassessing the relationship between value and representation through their writing.[13] Percy Bysshe Shelley, for example, critiqued the paper money economy in his radical 1819 poem, *The Masque of Anarchy*, written in protest against the Peterloo Massacre and the exploitation of the working class:

'Tis to let the Ghost of Gold
Take from Toil a thousandfold
More than e'er its substance could
In the tyrannies of old.

Paper Coin—that forgery
Of the title-deeds which ye
Hold to something of the worth
Of the inheritance of the Earth.[14]

Decrying the corruption of coin by paper, Shelley's poem demands legal reform in response to the forgery trials and what the Scottish lawyer, Henry Brougham, described as the 'moral revolution' created by the prosecutions.[15]

Jane Austen's novels are equally responsive to the crisis of representation caused by the Restriction Period and carefully capture the move from an economy grounded by landed property to a speculative economy of circulating paper. Earlier eighteenth-century novels like Henry Fielding's *Tom Jones* (1749), in contrast to the currency it-narratives, anxiously reject circulating paper currency in favour of the stability of landed property. Austen's novels, however, become increasingly mobile, moving from the security offered by Pemberley in *Pride and Prejudice* (1813) to the exciting temptation of the sea and naval life in *Persuasion* (1817), while her unfinished novel, *Sanditon* (written in 1817), begins with a carriage accident that symbolises an unmoored speculative economy moving too fast. Her novels give us glimpses of a transition into market speculation, which the sociologist Max Weber would later famously argue, 'reaches its full significance only from the moment property takes on the form of negotiable paper'.[16] Austen's novels teach her readers not only the importance of careful close reading in choosing a worthy husband in the marriage economy, but also confront the speculative disasters caused by gossip left unchallenged in *Northanger Abbey* (1817) and *Sanditon*; the miscalculations caused by the spectacularly bad social reader, Emma; and the corrupting taint of imperial expansion and slavery in *Mansfield Park* (1814). Austen, therefore, asks her readers to move beyond the face-value judgement of articles of exchange and to instead consider the social and emotional implications of economic interactions. Implications that she was keenly aware of given the calamitous failure of her brother Henry's bank in 1816.

As Britain's economy became increasingly marked by financial bubbles and crashes in the nineteenth century, its novels became equally populated with fraudsters, detectives, bankers, speculative misdeeds, and infectious economies. Consider, for example, the way Charles Dickens describes the epidemic of speculation gripping the characters in *Little Dorrit* (1855–57) following the rise of the banker (and as of yet, undiscovered fraudster), Mr Merdle:

> That it is at least as difficult to stay a moral infection as a physical one; that such a disease will spread with the malignity and rapidity of the Plague; that the contagion, when it has once made head, will spare no pursuit or condition, but will lay hold on people in the soundest health, and become developed in the most unlikely constitutions; is a fact as firmly established by experience as that we human creatures breathe an atmosphere ... As a vast fire will fill the air to a great distance with its roar, so the sacred flame which the mighty Barnacles had fanned caused the air to resound more and more, with the name of Merdle. It was deposited on every lip, and carried into every ear. There never was, there never had been, there never again

should be, such a man as Mr. Merdle. Nobody, as aforesaid, knew what he had done; but everybody knew him to be the greatest that had appeared.[17]

With one of its early scenes opening in a Marseille quarantine following an outbreak of infectious diseases and one of its final scenes depicting the gothicised collapse of the Clenham banking house—eaten away by whispers and rumours in the walls, as the final chapter titles take on the narrative chime of an auction (Going, Going!, Gone)—*Little Dorrit* is the contagion narrative that Robert Shiller should have turned to in *Narrative Economics* (2019) to illustrate and understand the power of economic narratives to spread, corrode, and collapse.

Wilkie Collins' sensationalist novel, *The Moonstone* (1868) equally depicts a fever of speculation: this time a detective fever (itself a speculative activity) takes hold of its characters as they try to solve the mystery of the moonstone diamond (its origins, value, and disappearance): ' "Do you feel an uncomfortable heat at the pit of your stomach, sir? and a nasty thumping at the top of your head? Ah! not yet? It will lay hold of you . . . I call it the detective-fever" '.[18] Speculative crises multiply as multiple narratives fight to dominate and fix *their* status as accurate, involving the reader in the detective fever of speculation as we read and judge each separate narrative's value and veracity, determined to solve the mystery ourselves. Anthony Trollope's *The Way We Live Now* (1875) also overwhelms its reader with competing types of circulating paper. Like Dickens' Mr Merdle, Trollope's fraudulent speculator, Mr Melmotte commits suicide as the novel becomes awash with valueless paper: letters, IOUs, worthless railway stock, and dinner tickets to Melmotte's extravagant party all become caught in an inflationary bubble until the burst that registers again the fissure between representation and value. A fissure that literature is at pains to emphasise and that economics so frequently ignores.

Reading Future Failures

The reiterative deferral of payment necessitated by the Restriction Act ('promises to pay promises with promises') demonstrates that money is what Lana Swartz terms an 'instrument of shared temporality' or as Bill Maurer argues value and money are 'conjured in relation to pasts remembered, futures anticipated, and time measured'.[19] 'We accept something as money', Swartz argues, 'because we expect that it will be accepted tomorrow'.[20] The Bank Restriction Period, therefore, cleaved open the double meaning of the word 'currency' as both a medium of monetary exchange and a term that denotes prevalence and acceptance, demonstrating the unfixed nature of monetary currency: how it can undergo temporal shifts in which it can either gain or lose currency; how it is always dependent on a recipient willing to recognise and guarantee its value. Cruikshank's note illustrated the potential human costs of the fallibility and temporality of the Bank of England's currency: the 'During . . . and until

Resumption' inscription indicates the interrupted trust of shared temporality created by the Restriction Period—a suspension not only of convertibility but of a shared understanding of value's past, present, and future.

On 27 February 1797, the paper currency of the Bank of England was both enshrined and lost. More than two centuries later, the Irish novelist Deirdre Madden would trace a similar overnight betrayal by national financial institutions and governments through the 'bank guarantee' and the 'spectacular economic crash' of Ireland that followed. In her aptly titled novel, *Time Present and Time Past* (2013), Madden plays with the fragile temporality of currency. Opening in the spring of 2006, Madden rushes the closing of her novel to a future past, 'What is going to happen in Ireland at the end of the first decade of the twenty-first century has been so exhaustively reported elsewhere as to not need significant comment here'. Yet her narrator nonetheless continues:

> All the citizens of Ireland will be asleep. Government ministers will have to be woken from their beds to go and take part in this historical event. The people of Ireland . . . will wake one morning some two years hence, and turning on their radios, will be stunned to discover that during the night the heads of all the major banks have gone to the government and obliged it to honour all of the banks' considerable debts. People will think they must be imagining things; that they must still be asleep and dreaming, but no: it is a fact . . . Things will get worse and worse, leading a couple of years later, at the end of the decade, to the intervention of the external agencies and the loss of economic sovereignty. This would be traumatic for any democracy, but is felt particularly keenly in Ireland, given its history.[21]

In this brief passage towards the close of her novel, Madden draws on the various temporalities of Ireland's colonial history, its emergence as an independent sovereign state, its financial exuberance during the Celtic Tiger years, and its future-past financial collapse to narrate a single family's history, while also expressing the cultural role of money in narrating that history. Although centred on the Irish experience of the Global Financial Crisis of 2008/9, Madden manipulates the narrative time in the novel through the *projection* of a future past; the trade in narrative futures the novel enacts; the disaster of futures *not* anticipated—and the implicit references to the failed promises of the bank guarantee—such that the novel's projected financial crisis has significant resonances elsewhere, in particular to the trade in derivatives that was at the centre of the GFC.[22]

In his study of the role derivatives played in the 2008 financial crisis, cultural theorist Arjun Appadurai draws on anthropologist Marcel Mauss' theory of the gift and philosopher J. L. Austin's work on the performative speech act of the promise (when you say, 'I promise', you *perform* the act of promising) to demonstrate that the GFC was primarily caused by a 'failure of language'. He argues that the collapse of derivative markets that occurred in 2008 was about 'failed promises': a 'failure that was neither occasional nor ad hoc but became systematic and contagious, thus bringing the entire financial market to the brink of disaster'. Derivatives are assets that *derive* their value from other assets in an indefinitely long chain such that

> the derivative is above all a linguistic phenomenon, since it is primarily a referent to something more tangible than itself: it is a proposition or a belief about another object that might itself be similarly derived from yet another similar object.

Emphasising the abstract nature of the derivative market, Appadurai argues that the 'derivative's claim to value is essentially linguistic' because the derivative's value chain 'has no status other than the credibility of their reference to something more tangible than themselves'.[23] This chain of deferred value, therefore brings us back again to the promises paid with promises that haunted the Bank Restriction Period and underscores that the force of the derivative's value is 'primarily performative'—'tied up with context, convention, and felicity'—that also returns us to the instruments of shared temporality. The trade in derivatives was essentially a hedge on whether the shared temporality evoked by currency would continue or not, with bets placed on both sides, and bets placed on those bets, *ad nauseam*.

The market in derivatives therefore heightens the crisis of representation attached to currency, pushing money to its most abstract form, its 'highest technical expression' as a 'manmade symbolic object':

> The derivative, which is primarily a way to take a risk on a prior risk, opens the prospect of making money whether the future price of an asset *goes up or down*. This last point is vital, for derivatives traders can make (or lose) money whether underlying prices for assets go up or go down at the end of any particular time interval. This makes risk-taking in the derivatives market independent of the real course of commodity values in the real world of goods and services.[24]

The 'problematic of representation' associated with paper currency divorced from the value of bullion therefore balloons in the derivative market as its value becomes purely *derivative*. One of the few concrete referents a derivative was seemingly tied to, and gained its credibility from, was the housing market. As the GFC showed, however, the property market and the trade in mortgages it entails is equally subject to abstraction, chains of referents, and circulating paper through the amortisation of home loans (the repayment of a debt over a significant period of time, usually decades long). What seems to distinguish the housing market, as Appadurai argues, is the socio-cultural belief in property as the ultimate stable investment, a sign of 'financial adulthood and security'; despite the fact that you only own a piece of paper, you are taught to believe that you own a home. This creates for Appadurai a 'bizarre materiality' in which, although the

> visible material form [of the mortgaged home] is relatively fixed, bounded, and indivisible, its financial form, the mortgage, has now been structured to be endlessly divisible, recombinable, saleable, and leverage-able for financial speculators in a manner that is both mysterious and toxic.[25]

The distinction between the valorised landed property and the speculative circulating paper currency of the eighteenth century, therefore, completely collapses in the derivative market of mortgages.

Turning to another Irish novel centred on the Celtic Tiger crash illustrates the devastating social costs of the GFC and the 'bizarre materiality' that turns a home into a 'mysterious and toxic' speculation. Set in regional Ireland post-Celtic Tiger, Donal Ryan's 2012 novel, *The Spinning Heart* illuminates the myriad tragedies experienced by a single community following the crash through multiple first-person narrations. All the characters become in some manner entangled with the consequences of a failed housing estate caused by the property developer, Pokey Burke, going 'bust' due to his investments 'into some stupid thing to do with a fake island or something out in Dubai'.[26] Sardonically labelled, 'Pokey Burke's estate of horrors' by one of the character-narrators of the novel, the ghost estate embodies the failed bank guarantee, exposes the chinks in the chain of mortgage derivatives, and illuminates the spectral nature of financial abstraction. Fittingly, Pokey Burke is nowhere to be found in the Tipperary town, having fled his creditors, and is equally a spectral figure in the narration, not given a speaking part in the novel, with the reader only catching glimpses of him through other characters' narrative experience. Ryan's 'haunted' estate recalls Marx's gothicisation of capitalism and his determination to reveal the secret of a commodity's value discussed in Chapter 1. Like Marx, Ryan is equally determined to show the community of labouring bodies tied to the value of property and what gets erased through this abstraction and transformation of property into tradable currencies. Many of Ryan's narrators are former builders (or their family members) who worked for Burke and have lost not only their jobs, but also their social security benefits due to Burke's dishonest business dealings. In focusing on these characters and their economic, familial, social, and ethical crises, Ryan demands that his readers trace what the French philosopher, Jacques Derrida (following Marx), described as a 'certain haunting' of capitalism. The ghostly 'estate of horrors' illuminates Derrida's 'spectral movement of this [commodity] chain', allowing readers to give themselves up to the 'invisibility' of capitalism and 'to see, at first sight, what does not let itself be seen': the abstraction of a home's labour value.[27] The novel therefore refuses to allow the bank guarantee to remain as an economic abstraction of a failed promise (the Irish government's hedge on the future value of the Irish banks), but the failure to secure the livelihoods of citizens.

Tokens of Value

Since the collapse of the global financial market in 2008/9, money has seemingly become even more abstract, decentralised, and representational. Following this trend, the famous board game Monopoly, once a banking microcosm of trading property for cash payments in the form of paper currency, has now moved into the financial realm of electronic payments, with even one of its children's versions replacing paper money with bank cards and an 'electronic banking unit' while the 'voice banking' family version boasts that there 'is no need for bank or cash cards' as 'The Mr Monopoly banking unit [modelled on the famous tophat] manages all finances whether it's buying properties, paying and receiving rent, checking balances and more'.[28] The Monopoly transition captures the ways in which digital cultures are wielding increasing power in the financial market. What is traditionally understood as money is 'being replaced' by what Rachel O'Dwyer defines as 'online tokens':

> digital platforms are issuing new kinds of money-like things [not just non-fungible tokens (NFTs)], from airtime to loyalty, gift vouchers, game tokens, and customer data. Tokens are now used to turn invisible stuff into assets, to pay wages, to track purchases, and to programme and specify the terms of financial access and inclusion.[29]

Tokens, as O'Dwyer acknowledges, are not new. They have long circulated and kept company with money as a means of 'trad[ing] against stored assets; [paying] wages for everything from jury duty to sex work' and as a way of granting 'access to secret societies'. Tokens have been used 'to pay for wars and infrastructure; to remember; to credit; to keep account'. What is new, however, is the rate at which token use is rising and replacing traditional forms of monetary currency. Citing examples of Amazon paying some of its workers through Amazon gift cards, or how mobile airtime has become a tradable currency in many regions of the Global South, O'Dwyer argues that while tokens can perform many of the functions money does, such as 'store value, buy things, and pay wages', they nonetheless 'blur the hard edges between legitimate and illegitimate work and legitimate and illegitimate transactions' with the backgrounds of many of these token-issuing companies to be found in the gaming or social media industries rather than the financial sector: 'Most [of these companies] don't even have a financial licence'.[30] This highlights the potential of tokens to be used subversively as well as illegally; operating outside the confines of the national banking system, online tokens are not subject to the same regulatory frameworks that the traditional monetary systems are supposedly governed by.

If payment is, as Swartz compellingly argues, 'a form of communication' and a 'way of transmitting information that produces shared meaning' or 'a *transactional community*', then the rise of un/under-regulated tokens raises difficult questions about how inclusive, or indeed, exclusive these *tokenised* communities of payment are?[31] O'Dwyer's example of the trade in phone airtime is taken to terrifying prospects in the speculative fiction, *Moxyland* (2008), by South African novelist Lauren Beukes who imagines a future Cape Town under the thrall of biotech and surveillance technology where being disconnected from your mobile phone means that you are exiled from society, have no rights to health care or public transport, and are stripped of your access to money. In a revisioning of South African Apartheid, being 'disconnect' means 'No phone. No service. No life'.[32] In Beukes' fictionalised world of hyper-surveillance the separation between the online world (of video games and cyber sabotage) and reality collapses: online interactions are tracked, manipulated, and monetised for the state's gain; advertising is embedded in the epidermis through biotech; and skin cells are scraped for contractual signatures. The epidermis and its DNA become tokens.

Outside Beukes' speculative fiction, personal data *can and is* tokenised— as 'value-transfer layer[s]' tokens can 'turn invisible stuff into assets'.[33] In the recent cyberattack that collapsed the digital infrastructure of the British Library, the personal data of staff and library members quickly became a form of an online token that could be traded on the dark web. While the digital infrastructure of the Library may appear ephemeral, its collapse completely halted the access to its physical repositories (books, maps, archives, and manuscripts) for months. Nor can the impact caused by the disruption of access to its online databases (such as journals and newspapers) be underestimated: the knowledge economy attached to the Library has completely crumbled. As the Bodleian's Librarian at Oxford, Richard Ovenden explains: 'This cyberattack on the Library highlights both the vulnerability of the digital world, and the crucial importance of knowledge in modern Britain' and beyond, as 'the media coverage has overlooked the role the Library plays as a crucial node in the global network of knowledge'.[34] Although it is hard to measure the financial cost of this cyberattack on the global knowledge economy that is already facing major assaults through attempts at censorship, funding cuts, and political interventions, the Library now faces a costly rebuild of its infrastructure and a bill of almost £7m after it refused to pay the £600,000 ransom demanded by the attackers. As digital tokens proliferate, so does the digital vulnerability to financial collapse.

The subversive potential of tokens can, however, also work in the opposite direction, to build and protect communities. Part of the appeal of cryptocurrencies, such as Bitcoin or Ether (the cryptocurrency of the Ethereum blockchain), is the notion that they are more democratic and subject to far less state surveillance and corruption than national currencies. Fuelled by a distrust in national banks, cryptocurrencies have surged in popularity since the GFC

Currency 63

and the bailout of banks that followed it. Analysing what she terms Bitcoin's 'techno-economic imaginaries', Swartz argues that for its original supporters (cypherpunks and crypto-anarchists) the cryptocurrency promotes the self-sovereignty of individuals as it is a 'self-sovereign' currency. Its decentralisation from national banks also provides its users with a model of privacy that could potentially support 'collective autonomy', where Bitcoin's blockchain (the digital ledger that ensures that the currency cannot be manipulated or corrupted) is seen as a 'cooperative infrastructure' that should be 'maintained for the collective good'. The anarchic potential of Bitcoin, and cryptocurrencies in general, has however, undergone its own corruption as the 'hobbyist' or artisanal miner of 'digital gold' was replaced by industrial miners and that digital mining has itself become 'an act of speculation' where 'those prospecting for digital gold engaged in a technological arms race in mining equipment' that ultimately destroyed the 'mutalist infrastructure' of the blockchain. Pushed out by the monopolies of scale involved in digital mining industrialisation, the potential of the self-sovereign miner was quickly and completely undermined.[35] Mining pools—where miners combine or 'pool' their computational resources to mine on a larger scale—have taken over, with a 2020 report concluding that five companies based in China controlled almost half of 'Bitcoin's computing power'.[36] As O'Dwyer argues, 'Technology is never neutral. Who shapes it and what it does have political consequences.'[37] The monopolies created by mining pools undermines the decentralisation that was at the heart of Bitcoin's initial appeal and success, disrupting the techno-imaginary of sovereign individuality it promised.

One of the most fascinating elements of the cryptocurrency techno-imaginary is its dependency on the materiality of an extractive imaginary and the continued reliance on and a socio-cultural attachment to the materiality of currency. The physical tokens created as 'real' monetary representations of cryptocurrencies—combining metals such as brass, silver, and gold with an embedded digital code—capture the slippage between value and representation this chapter began with. Meme currencies such as the Dogecoin created to capitalise on the popularity of the meme of the confused and disgruntled looking Shiba Inu dog (2013 meme of the year), while seemingly created as a 'joke' nonetheless had an exponential rise of 26,000 percent over a 6-month period in 2021.[38] Collapsing the online and physical world of tokens into each other the physical manifestation of Dogecoins created by the company Cryptochips offers its customers a choice of gold or silver with the minted image of Doge surrounded by the meme-worthy legend: 'MUCH WOW TO THE MOON WE GO DECENTRALISED PEER-TO-PEER DIGITAL CURRENCY—ONE DOGE'. While emphasising the craftsmanship of the coins and that iron gives the coin its 'signature weight', the company is nonetheless clear to specify in its FAQs that 'all crypto merch produced by Cryptochips are meant for novelty purposes only and do not contain any digital value to them'.[39] Instead of the weight of the metallic coin being the standard bearer of value here (such as the attic standard of the Athenian Tetradrachms in the ancient Greek world), the physical coin has no value in the digital realm of currencies.[40] A fake story about a man's arrest for selling Chuck E. Cheese tokens as Bitcoins that went viral in 2017 shows how blurred the lines are between digital and material currencies in the cultural imaginary of cryptocurrencies.[41] Even in the virtual world of digital-currency Monopoly we find the metonymic material impulse as Mr Monopoly's top hat stands in for the bank with all the associated metaphorical implications: class status, gentlemanly trust, and institutional stability, but with debt collection quickly due with a flip of the hat.

Despite celebrating its digital nativism, Bitcoin's explanatory narrative is likewise fastened to the material and to the traditional and romanticised story of mining. Promotional videos for Bitcoin animate the digital currency's 'mining' through icons of pick-axes and shovels, while the actual 'digital mining' is illustrated as an individual striking a piece of rock which produces a gold-encrusted Bitcoin even while it is connected to an animation of a data centre. It has a videogame aesthetic that emphasises the gaming aspect of Bitcoin mining.[42] The language of physical resource mining proliferates too: the computer processors required to perform the mathematical calculations that unlock Bitcoins are referred to as 'mining rigs'; the currencies are described as 'finite resources' (thereby bolstering their perceived value); cryptocurrencies have been deemed digital 'blood diamonds' for their use in illegal transactions and their popularity on the dark web. Drawing a comparison between Bitcoin's 'digital architecture' and the sixteenth-century silver mining economy of Cerro Rico de Potosí in South America, the literary historian Zac Zimmer argues that 'Bitcoin's mining metaphor is in fact a felicitous one, as it paints a clear image of the ideology behind the Bitcoin moment'. Urging us 'to pay attention to the logic of extraction hardcoded into the blockchain's very essence', Zimmer concludes that 'the techno-utopianism surrounding this global digital currency' quickly 'dissolve[s] into a dystopian realm of scarcity and misery, buried deep within the infernal depths of the earth'.[43] Like the evocative image painted in Chrysal the guinea's extraction from the earth by the gold miner, cryptocurrency miners are entrenched in a system of digging for scarce resources.

Regardless of the utopian promotional material that accompanies Bitcoin and other cryptocurrencies, Zimmer is clear that digital mining is nonetheless a 'terraforming operation' and part of the process of 'digital primitive accumulation': 'The blockchain can be more accurately understood as terraforming the digital financial realm, rather than decentralizing it. Bitcoin is cryptoforming the Internet, with the goal of transitioning the financial sphere into an environment of digital metalism'.[44] The environmental costs of cryptocurrency mining are stark. A 2022 report by specialists in digital and energy finance estimated that 'Bitcoin mining may be responsible for 65.4 megatonnes of CO_2 (MtCO2) per year' which, they argue, is 'comparable to country-level emissions in Greece'.[45] A UN report concluded that 'if Bitcoin were a country, its energy consumption would have ranked 27th in the world, ahead of a country like Pakistan, with a population of over 230 million people'. To offset Bitcoin mining's carbon footprint would require the planting of 3.9 billion trees, while the cryptocurrency's water footprint was 'enough to meet the current domestic water needs of more than 300 million people in rural sub-Saharan Africa'.[46] The digital cousins of cryptocurrency, generative artificial intelligence tools like ChatGPT share in this huge environmental cost. In an article for the *MIT Technology Review*, Karen Hao compared the AI industry to the oil industry: 'once mined and refined, data, like oil can be a highly lucrative commodity'; but also like its 'fossil-fuel counterpart, the process of deep learning has an outsize environmental impact' with the carbon footprint created by the life-cycle of training natural language processing amounting to almost five times that of the emissions created by an average American car across its lifetime.[47] The environmental costs associated with these industries also need to be combined with: the costs to creatives through the concerted attempts to undermine their copyright, and the ethical price of privacy concerns given how data hungry generative AI processes are.[48] The terraforming operations and potential corruptions by data centres are perhaps best illustrated by an Irish case study: the peat landslide caused by the construction of the Meenbog Wind Farm, which as Patrick Brodie has demonstrated, had 'sold its future energy to global logistics and cloud giant Amazon Web Services (AWS) to power its data center operations in Dublin'.[49] Thus the green transition and decarbonisation efforts have been co-opted into the infrastructures of an energy-hungry digital future where 'data centre energy consumption in 2021 accounted for 14% of electricity nationally [in Ireland], with rural households accounting for 12%'.[50]

***

The confronting image of the land literally crumbling to the weight of a wind farm created to support the energy infrastructures of the digital economy emphasises not only the ceaseless imbrication of the material and the digital, but also demonstrates the multiple erosions of trust on which currency's future-oriented temporality and imaginary relies. As currencies and tokens proliferate globally, the community of currency seems more disparate than ever and the image of Pitt sitting astride the Bank of England defecating seemingly valueless paper money could perhaps be easily replaced by the digital giants squatting on a windfarm on a bog in Ireland as the land gives way.

Notes

1 Bank of England, *Bank of England, February 27th, 1797: In Consequence of an Order of His Majesty's Privy Council Notified to the Bank Last Night* (London: Gale, 1797, Eighteenth Century Collections Online).

66 *Currency*

2 Phil Handler, 'Forging the Agenda: The 1819 Select Committee on Criminal Laws Revisited', *The Journal of Legal History* 25, no. 3 (2004), 249–268 (252).
3 Phil Handler, 'Forgery and the End of the "Bloody Code" in Early Nineteenth-Century England', *The Historical Journal* 48, no. 3 (2005), 683–702 (690). See, also, Ian Haywood, *Romanticism and Caricature* (Cambridge: Cambridge University Press, 2013).
4 See Curator's Notes for Bank Restriction Note, Object Number 1978, U.955, British Museum, https://www.britishmuseum.org/collection/object/P_1978-U-955
5 William Cobbett, *Paper Against Gold; or, the History and Mystery of the Bank of England, of the Debt, of the Stocks, of the Sinking Fund, and of the Other Tricks and Contrivances, carried on by the Means of Paper Money* (London: W. M. Cobbett, 1828).
6 Kevin Barry, 'The Aesthetics of Paper Money: National Differences During the Period of Enlightenment and Romanticism', in *Scotland, Ireland, and the Romantic Aesthetic*, ed. David Duff and Catherine Jones (Lewisburg: Bucknell University Press, 2007), 55–76 (55).
7 Mary Poovey, *Genres of the Credit Economy: Mediating Value in Eighteenth- and Nineteenth-Century Britain* (Chicago: University of Chicago Press, 2008), 5.
8 Lana Swartz, *New Money: How Payment Became Social Media* (New Haven: Yale University Press, 2020), 27.
9 Charles Johnstone, *Chrysal; or the Adventures of a Guinea* (London, 1760).
10 Thomas Bridges, *The Adventures of a Bank-Note: In Two Volumes* (London: T. Davies, 1770–1771), 5.
11 Poovey, *Genres of the Credit Economy*, 146–147.
12 Christopher Flint, 'Speaking Objects: The Circulation of Stories in Eighteenth-Century Prose Fiction', *PMLA* 113, no. 2 (1998), 212–226 (224); Aileen Douglas, 'Britannia's Rule and the It-Narrator', *Eighteenth-Century Fiction* 6, no. 1 (1993), 65–82 (71).
13 See, for example, Sheryl Craig, *Jane Austen and the State of the Nation* (Basingstoke: Palgrave Macmillan, 2015); Alexander Dick, *Romanticism and the Gold Standard: Money, Literature, and Economic Debate in Britain 1790–1830* (Basingstoke: Palgrave Macmillan, 2013); Mary Poovey, 'From Politics to Silence: Jane Austen's Nonreferential Aesthetic', *Companion to Jane Austen*, ed. Claudia L. Johnson and Clara Tuite (Oxford: Blackwell Publishing, 2009), 249–260.
14 Percy Bysshe Shelley, *Shelley's Poetry and Prose*, ed. Donald A. Reiman and Neil Freistat (New York: Norton, 2002), 321, ll. 176–183.
15 See Dick, *Romanticism and the Gold Standard*, especially, 110–149.
16 Max Weber, *General Economic History*, trans. Frank Knight (Mineola: Dover Publishing, Inc., 2003), 278.
17 Charles Dickens, *Little Dorrit*, ed. Harvey Peter Sucksmith and intro. Dennis Walder (Oxford: Oxford University Press, 2012), 560.
18 Wilkie Collins, *The Moonstone*, ed. Francis O'Gorman (Oxford: Oxford University Press, 2019), 294.

Currency 67

19 Lana Swartz, 'What Was Bitcoin, What Will It Be? The Techno-Economic Imaginaries of a New Money Technology', *Cultural Studies* 32, no. 4 (2018), 623–650 (624); Bill Maurer, *Mutual Life, Limited: Islamic Banking, Alternative Currencies, Lateral Reasoning* (Princeton: Princeton University Press, 2005), 89.
20 Swartz, 'What Was Bitcoin', 624.
21 Deirdre Madden, *Time Present and Time Past* (London: Faber and Faber, 2013), 199–200.
22 Failed promises because 'the banks were mendacious in their dealings with the government on that night, and their debts are far greater than was then admitted to' (Madden, *Time Present and Time Past*, 200) thereby tying the government's future spending to the enormous debts amounted by the banks in the past.
23 Arjun Appadurai, *Banking on Words: The Failure of Language in the Age of Derivative Finance* (Chicago: University of Chicago Press, 2016), 2–4.
24 Appadurai, *Banking on Words*, 12.
25 Appadurai, *Banking on Words*, 61.
26 Donal Ryan, *The Spinning Heart* (London: Penguin, 2019), 43.
27 Jacques Derrida, *Specters of Marx: The State of the Debt, the Work of Mourning and the New International* (New York: Routledge, 2006), 187.
28 'Monopoly Voice Banking', Amazon, https://www.amazon.co.uk/Monopoly-Junior/dp/B07SZRHWYY?th=1
29 Rachel O'Dwyer, *Tokens: The Future of Money in the Age of the Platform* (London: Verso, 2023), 9.
30 O'Dwyer, *Tokens*, 9, 11.
31 Swartz, *New Money*, 16.
32 Lauren Beukes, *Moxyland* (Johannesburg: Jacana Media, 2008), 17.
33 O'Dwyer, *Tokens*, 9.
34 Richard Ovenden, 'The British Library Hack Is a National Outrage– and the Government Must Pay to Save It', *The Standard*, 19 January 2024, https://www.standard.co.uk/comment/british-library-cyber-hack-government-funding-b1133220.html
35 Swartz, 'What Was Bitcoin', 629–634.
36 Amy Castor, 'Report: Mining Pool Consolidation Threatens Bitcoin Security', *Modern Consensus*, 4 February 2020, https://modernconsensus.com/cryptocurrencies/bitcoin/report-mining-pool-consolidation-threatens-bitcoin-security/
37 O'Dwyer, *Tokens*, 12.
38 MacKenzie Sigalos, 'How Dogecoin Went from a Joke to One of the World's Top Currencies', *CNBC*, 7 May 2021, https://www.cnbc.com/2021/05/07/what-is-dogecoin.html; Stephen Hutcheon, 'The Rise and Rise of Dogecoin, the Internet's Hottest Cryptocurrency', *Sydney Morning Herald*, 24 Januarary 2014, https://www.smh.com.au/technology/the-rise-and-rise-of-dogecoin-the-internets-hottest-cryptocurrency-20140124-31d24.html
39 'Dogecoin', *Crypotchips*, https://www.cryptochips.io/products/dogecoin?_pos=1&_sid=721413358&_ss=r
40 Although tetradrachms could be subject to debasement through clipping, the attic standard was generally considered a stable monetary standard in Ancient Greece. See, for example, Glyn Davies, *History of Money*

(Cardiff: University of Wales Press, 2005); Philip L. Cottrell, Gérassimos Notaras, and Gabriel Tortella, eds., *From the Athenian Tetradrachm to the Euro: Studies in European Monetary Integration* (Aldershot: Ashgate Publishing Company, 2007).

41 The fake story claimed that a man in the United States was arrested after making a million dollars selling the entertainment company Chuck E. Cheese tokens as Bitcoins. First 'reported' on a satirical website, Huzlers, the story gained popularity through social media as people relished in the idea of the success of fake 'real' Bitcoins and was later debunked by a number of news agencies, including the *San Diego Union-Tribune*: Taylor Rock, 'That Chuck E. Cheese Bitcoin Deal Is Fake News', *San Diego Union-Tribune*, 17 December 2017, https://www.sandiegouniontribune.com/lifestyle/food-and-cooking/sns-dailymeal-1863594-eat-chuck-e-cheese-bitcoin-fake-news-121917-20171219-story.html. Many thanks to Nathan K. Hensley for first bringing this story to my attention.
42 Bitcoinmining, https://www.bitcoinmining.com/.
43 Zac Zimmer, 'Bitcoin and Potosí Silver: Historical Perspectives on Cryptocurrency', *Technology and Culture* 58, no. 2 (2017), 307–334 (329).
44 Zimmer, 'Bitcoin and Potosí Silver', 326.
45 Alex de Vries et al., 'Revisiting Bitcoin's Carbon Footprint', *Joule* 6, no. 3 (2022), 498–502 (499).
46 Sanaz Chamanara, S. Arman Ghaffarizadeh, and Kaveh Madani, 'The Environmental Footprint of Bitcoin Mining Across the Globe: Call for Urgent Action', *Earth's Future* 11 (2023), 1–8.
47 Karen Hao, 'Training a Single AI Model can Emit as Much Carbon as Five Cars in their Lifetimes', *MIT Technology Review*, 6 June 2019, https://www.technologyreview.com/2019/06/06/239031/training-a-single-ai-model-can-emit-as-much-carbon-as-five-cars-in-their-lifetimes/
48 Sara Morrison, 'The Tricky Truth About How Generative AI Uses Your Data', *Vox*, 27 July 2023, https://www.vox.com/technology/2023/7/27/23808499/ai-openai-google-meta-data-privacy-nope
49 Patrick Brodie, 'Emerald Extractivism: Borders, Energy, and Data Infrastructures in Ireland', Selected Papers of AoIR2022, https://spir.aoir.org/ojs/index.php/spir/article/view/12979/10860
50 Patrick Bresnihan and Patrick Brodie, 'From Toxic Industries to Green Extractivism: Rural Environmental Struggles, Multinational Corporations and Ireland's Postcolonial Ecological Regime', *Irish Studies Review* 32, no. 1 (2024), 93–122 (99).

Index

Anthropocene 42–43
Appadurai, Arjun 58–60
artificial intelligence 65
Austen, Jane 1, 56

Bank of England 51–55, 58, 65
Bank Restriction Act 1797 5, 51, 54
Becker, Gary 35
behavioural economics 5, 37
Bentham, Jeremy 13, 20
Beukes, Lauren 62
Bitcoin 5, 62–65
Bridges, Thomas 54–55
British Library 62
Bulstrode, Jenny 42

Capitalocene 42
Celtic Tiger 58, 60
Chakrabarty, Dipesh 43
Charusheela, S. 38
Cobbett, William 54
Collins, Wilkie 57
Cort, Henry 42
Cruikshank, George 53–55
cryptocurrencies 5, 62–64

degrowth 5, 46–47
derivatives 58–60
Derrida, Jacques 60
Dickens, Charles 12, 37, 56, 57
Dogecoin 63

Edgeworth, Maria 12, 36

Feiner, Susan F. 36
feminist economics 5, 36
Ferguson, Niall 37
Fielding, Henry 56
Friedman, Milton 5, 20, 25–28

Gaskell, Elizabeth 37
Gillray, James 51, 52
Global Financial Crisis (GFC) 4, 5, 58–62
Global South 45, 46, 61
Great Convergence 4, 5, 45–46
Great Divergence 4, 5, 44–45
Greenspan, Alan 35
Green transition 65

Harvey, David 26, 46
Hayek, Friedrich von 5, 15, 20, 25–26
Homo economicus 5, 7, 33–38, 43, 44

identity economics 37
Industrial Revolution 5, 41–42, 46
Ingram, John Kells 14
it-narratives 54–55

James, Henry 20
Jevons, William Stanley 5, 18–20
Johnstone, Charles 55
jurisprudence 7, 10, 12, 34

Keynes, John Maynard 5, 21, 22–27, 34–35
Krugman, Paul 4

liberalism 26–28

Madden, Deirdre 58
Malthus, Thomas 5, 12, 24, 39–41
Marcet, Jane 12–13, 14
marginal revolution 12, 18–20
Marshall, Alfred 15, 18, 20–23, 34
Martineau, Harriet 12
Marx, Karl 5, 12, 15–18, 44, 45, 60
Maurer, Bill 57
McCloskey, Deirdre 4, 10
Menger, Carl 18
Mill, John Stuart 5, 13–15, 18, 21, 25, 34–35, 40–41
monopoly (game) 61, 64
Moore, Jason 42
mortgage 59–60

neoclassical economics 12, 18, 20, 37, 45–46
neoliberalism 4, 26–27
novel 37, 55–57

O'Dwyer, Rachel 61–63

paper currency 51–55, 58–61
poetry 15, 36
Pomeranz, Kenneth 44
Poovey, Mary 54, 55
postcolonial economics 5, 37–38, 42
primitive accumulation 42, 45, 64

racial capitalism 42
Rand, Ayn 35
Reagan, Ronald 26, 35
Ricardo, David 4, 10–14, 17, 21, 23, 34, 40
Robinson, Cedric, J. 42
Ryan, Donal 60

Saad-Filho, Alfredo 45, 46
Shelley, Percy Bysshe 55–56
Shiller, Robert J. 4, 57
Short, Graham 1
slave trade 1, 37, 38, 45–46, 56
Smith, Adam 5, 7–13, 16–19, 22, 24, 25, 28, 33–34, 38
South Sea Bubble 1–3, 36
stadial theory 4, 5, 19, 38–39, 42, 44
stationary state 40–41
Swartz, Lana 57, 62, 63
Swift, Jonathan 36

Thatcher, Margaret 26
Torrens, Robert 12
Toynbee, Arnold 41
traditional ecological knowledge 43

Vidal, Gore 35

Walras, Léon 18
Ward, Edward 36
Whyte, Kyle 43
Woolf, Virginia 24
Wordsworth, William 14–15

Zein-Elabdin, Eiman O. 38
Zimmer, Zac 64

For Product Safety Concerns and Information please contact our EU
representative GPSR@taylorandfrancis.com
Taylor & Francis Verlag GmbH, Kaufingerstraße 24, 80331 München, Germany

www.ingramcontent.com/pod-product-compliance
Lightning Source LLC
Chambersburg PA
CBHW071823230426
43670CB00013B/2552